John White Chadwick

The Possible Life

And Other Sermons

John White Chadwick

The Possible Life
And Other Sermons

ISBN/EAN: 9783337116910

Printed in Europe, USA, Canada, Australia, Japan

Cover: Foto ©Lupo / pixelio.de

More available books at **www.hansebooks.com**

THE POSSIBLE LIFE

AND OTHER SERMONS

BY

JOHN W. CHADWICK

TWENTY-FIRST AND TWENTY-SECOND SERIES

BOSTON
GEO. H. ELLIS, 141 FRANKLIN STREET
1897

CONTENTS

TWENTY-FIRST SERIES.

TWENTY-SECOND SERIES.

THE PUBLIC SERVICE OF RELIGION.

It cannot be inappropriate for us, coming together as we do to-day after a period of separation, and about to enter on another year of common thought and work, to seriously consider why we are here, what business we have in hand, what justification there is for this religious institution, and for the more general institution of which this church of ours is an infinitesimal part. Mr. Balfour may be fully justified in his persuasion that men generally think and speak and act from habit and tradition and authority; but, when he adds "and not on reasonable grounds," we say: "Hold there! Are you quite sure of that?" May it not be that habit and tradition and authority hold a good deal of reason, as it were in solution; that they are to a considerable extent reason gone into structure; that reason is the kobold of Scandinavian folk-lore which cannot be shaken off, but mounts the cart of household goods, and goes with them wherever they go? They reckon ill who leave him out. When him they fly, he is the wings. There is no reason here for our abdication of the rights of reason and their habitual exercise. However much of reason is implicated in habit and tradition and authority, there is plenty of unreason, too, which demands the exercise of reason for its elimination. And though, doubtless, the days would not be long enough for the reasoning out of every principle or persuasion upon which we act, and we may well be thankful for the fund of traditional principles and persuasions which we each inherit, yet does it behoove us to be adding something to this stock by the application of our own minds to many things. If all our predecessors had been content "to take, and give not on again," the fund of rational authority would have been much smaller than it is now,— a mole-hill, not a mountain for us to mine and quarry in at will. And then, too, there are many traditional conceptions which are of reason all compact, but it is other men's reason ; and it makes a world of difference whether we open our mouths and shut our eyes in the hope of something to make us wise, or re-think what has been thought before, and make it ours as it was theirs who thought it out before us. We all of us believe that the earth is round, and that it is flattened at the poles, and that it revolves around the sun. But what a difference it makes if we know these things by hearsay or have followed up the lines of thought that lead to them ! There are a thousand similar things, and one of them is — going to church. The great majority go to church because other people go, or because their fathers and mothers went before them. But there is a better way. It is that of the New Testament writer when he said, " Let every man be fully persuaded in his own mind." I will not say that men had better cease from "the assembling of themselves together " than not be able to give a reasonable account of their assembling ; but I will say that, by so much as a man can give a reasonable account of his conduct, by so much is he more a man, entitled to his self-respect and to the respect of other rational beings.

And then, too, of this particular we are bound to take some earnest heed,— that the public ministration of religion is subjected in our time to such a challenge as it has not been subjected to for many a day, if ever in the world before. For it is not the challenge of the fool, who has said in his heart there is no God ; of the brutal sensualist, who is resolved to make sure of the only pleasures that appeal to him as worth pursuing ; or the prudent epicure, who proposes to make sure of the good things of the present in fit measure and proportion, so that, if nothing at all or nothing better should materialize beyond the veil, he shall have had his day ; or the sordid money-getter, who conceives that getting money is the chief end of man, the top and crown of all his possible success. If the religious institution and observance

of our time were subjected to no more serious challenge than
is sounded by these several instruments, there would be
much less occasion than there is now for those who are
heartily persuaded of the importance and reality of this institution and observance to consider their position, and ask
themselves if they can justify it to their perfect satisfaction
at the bar of reason, or even in that lower court where
common sense holds its serene assize. No: the most serious challenge of our religious institution and observance is
the tacit one that comes from an increasing multitude of
men and women of good intellectual and moral standing
who find themselves refraining more and more habitually
from the public ministration of religion. It is the existence
of a large and steadily enlarging body of earnest, thoughtful
people whom we respect and admire who seem to get along
without religion, at least without its public recognition and
support. That the two things are widely different I am well
enough aware. There are not many towns or villages, or
even cities, where a man cannot get better spiritual food
than is served upon the tables of the churches in his immediate vicinity. If it is sermons that they want, they can get
those of Channing and Parker and Martineau and Brooks;
and there is many a preacher whom it would be an impiety
to go and hear when one might stay at home and read such
words of strength and peace. And we have, especially on
the part of religious liberals, too much complacency rather
than too little sympathy in the treatment of religious institutions which we cannot approve. The Unitarian *in partibus
infidelium* is too ready to unloose his purse-strings for the
local church as such. If there is a man in the pulpit preaching from week to week good tidings of sincerity and hope and
cheer, that is another matter. But, when it comes to aiding
and abetting a ministration of religion in which you do not
believe or trust, there is something to be said for common
honesty and self-respect as well as for good-nature and the
desire to please one's neighbors or one's friends. With so
many worthy objects crying for sympathy and help, money is

not the stuff that one should scatter with a careless hand, and, least of all, to fertilize a field of noisome weeds. Moreover, it is not as if all the resources of the non-church-going multitude were exhausted when they have read the best words of the best preachers of religion. Especially

> "To one who has been long in city pent
> 'Tis very sweet to look into the fair
> And open face of heaven,— to breathe a prayer
> Full in the smile of the blue firmament."

It was never bluer than at the very moment when I was writing that a week ago, and the church bell was tolling with a sweet and lingering invitation which I did not heed. More worshipful for me to lift up mine eyes unto the hills from whence cometh my help, to see the great white clouds trailing their dusky shadows over them. And yet, again, the non-church-goer has the mighty poets, "in their misery dead," it may be, but in their power and grace and helpfulness alive forevermore, and the great thinkers of the ages, the good books of many kinds,— one, very little known, called the New Testament, which contains "the story of a man" that is very helpful and inspiring, and as little like "the old, old story" of our traditional Christianity as one story can be like another.

You will think I have forgotten what I would be at, and that I am entering an earnest plea for total abstinence from church-going and the cultivation of home worship and individualism in religion; but I am doing nothing of the kind. Only I would not willingly believe that non-church-going is coextensive with indifference to religion and with failure to respond to its peculiar influence and charm; and I am glad that, without any wilfulness or perversion of the facts, I am encouraged to believe that it is not; that it may be, that it often is, the preference of a higher to a lower way, of good thoughts to bad, of something helpful and inspiring to something hindering and depressing. At the same time I cannot, without wilful blindness, fail to see that indifference to the public ministration of religion has not everywhere and always this lofty character, does not everywhere and always mean this preference for the higher and the highest things. It means, and not infrequently, that the home-staying, church-neglecting people are persuaded that religion is something which they can get along without, and that, too, very comfortably and decently, without loss of any real good. And here, exactly here, is the challenge of their method and observance which those who are heartily persuaded of the reality and importance of religion and its common recognition are bound to give attention to at the present time, and that right earnestly. It is a very serious challenge. If religion is not the greatest thing in the world, but a mere superfluity or absurdity or impertinence, we want to know it. We do not want to be watering a stick in the desert when there are so many things that have in them a principle of life and growth, and well deserve all the abundance of our wells and springs. We do not want to be wasting precious time and money on a plant that has in it no real vitality, no perfectly sincere relation to the needs of human life. We want to quit ourselves like men; and we are not doing so if we cannot give a reason for the faith that is in us, and feel that we are making a good honest contribution to the spiritual commonwealth of man. As for myself, there are some other things that I could do to good purpose and with much enjoyment; and I should like to be about them if I have been following an *ignis fatuus* these thirty years.

But, though it may seem presumptuous to differ from so many of the wise and excellent who are persuaded of the unreality of religion or of the uselessness of its public recognition, I do not find myself inclined — no, not in the least degree — to be of their assembly. For one thing, I cannot look at the succession of the ages, and see what a tremendous part religion has been playing on the busy scene, without being convinced that here is something essential to the completeness of humanity, something so deeply implicated in its structure that it can no more be taken out of it with-

out destructive consequences than the bones can be taken
out of a man's body or his muscles be unstrung of every
quivering nerve. No other force or institution has played
such a stupendous part in human history, has reared such
splendid fanes, dominated such mighty nations and events,
inspired such hopes and fears.

I am perfectly aware of the deductions that must be made
from this account by the impartial critic. "O Liberty,"
cried Madame Roland, "how many crimes have been committed in thy name!" Yes, certainly, but not a tithe of
those that have been committed in the name of religion.
What superstitions and idolatries and persecutions have
been multiplied along her course! How often she has
blocked the path of civilization and checked the growth of
science and thrust back the births of intellect into the womb
of time! From none of these things must we avert our eyes.
We could not if we would, they are so thrust upon us. But,
if they were exhaustive of the measure of religion, could we
be less convinced than we are now of the fundamental
reality of that in which such things inhere? We might feel
obliged to think it something abominable, infernal, devilish,
and consequently to revise our theories of human nature, and
conclude that Augustine and Calvin and Edwards said no
worse of it than what is true. But they are not exhaustive
of the measure of religion, these cursed and abominable
things. They are the spots upon the sun. They are the
least dust of the balance as compared with the inspirations of
goodness, reverence, comfort, peace, heroism, sacrifice, trust,
long-suffering, patience, that have been as much a part of it
as warmth is of the sunlight and fragrance of the rose.
And, when we think of what religion has been in its total
manifestation, in its terror and its beauty, in its loveliness
and joy, in its strength to build, its energy to sway, its might
to set up and cast down, then might we not as rationally
believe that the art of government, the State, or the passion
for beauty, or the love of men and women for each other,
was something superficial, something that might have its day

and cease to be, as to believe these things of religion? It
may be subjected to incalculable transformations in the
future as it has been in the past, but they will not destroy
its identity nor bring upon its perpetuity the shadow of a
doubt.

But there is another way of looking at the matter and a
much higher one than this with which we are now done.
It is to consider religion not in its historic course, but in
its ideal significance. What is religion so considered? It
is man's sense of the power and mystery of universal life,
and his endeavor to convert this sense into a binding law of
life. It has not always been this; for this has a moral element,—the endeavor to convert the sense of universal power
and mystery into a binding law of life,—and there was no
such moral element in the beginnings of religion. Religion
and morality were originally two separate streams, one rising
in the contact of man's spirit with the mystery of nature
and the mystery of his own life, and the other in the con-
tacts between man and man; but long since the two streams
coalesced, and now you might as well endeavor to separate
them as to separate the waters of the Hudson and the Mohawk below their junction with each other. Here and there
you find an individual like Benvenuto Cellini or the last pious
defaulter whose religion seems to have no moral character,
and here and there you find a splendid ethical development
with no conscious lifting of the heart to God; but, in the
wide average of history and of our semi-civilization, the religious and the moral elements are inextricably interwoven.

Separated in theory they often are by moralists and theologians. So are the bones and muscles on the dissecting
table or in anatomical treatises; but in the living organism
they are mutually supporting and sustaining, and cannot be
torn asunder without the destruction of that unity in which
they both inhere. There are those who, because they were
originally separate, would keep them separate still; but
they have coalesced as naturally as two rivers winding to
the sea, and it would be as absurd to seek to isolate them

now as to seek to isolate the Hudson's or the Mohawk's streaming flood. At the first swelling of the waters they would reunite; and separate religion and morality as you will in theory or practice, given some inundation of the one or of the other, and they would rush together with a joy and welcome as when long-parted lovers reunite.

Whatever religion has been, this is what it is,—man's sense of his relation to the power and mystery of universal life, and his endeavor to convert that sense into a binding law of life. You might as well say that the "Valkyrie" or the "Defender," *par nobile sororum*, ought to be a raft or dug-out because the original water-craft was a raft or dug-out as to say that religion ought to be exclusively man's sense of nature's power and mystery because it was so once.

> " Pleads for itself the fact
> As unrepentant Nature leaves her every act."

Here is the "Valkyrie" or the "Defender,"— a fair miracle of flowing lines and bellying sails and glorious motion,— and here is religion as it has come to be in the course of half a million years of human toil and stress, contact of the human spirit with the outer and the inner mystery, contact of man with man in the oppositions and the sympathies of social life.

> " The highest is the measure of the man,
> And not the Kaffir, Hottentot, Malay,
> And such horn-handed breakers of the glebe,
> But Homer, Plato, Verulam."

The highest is the measure of the water-craft, the government, the social state, the domestic relation, the religion. Nor in the reasoning of this present time is there a grosser fallacy than the attempt, which is so common, to interpret this thing or that in the terms of its original endowment, and to tie it down to the significance of that.

Somehow, by God's grace and man's, the raft or dug-out has become the ocean steamer and the yacht. Somehow, by

God's grace and man's, religion has become the twofold
energy of a divine and human inspiration, the twofold response of human nature to the All-embracer, the All-enfolder,
and to the obligations of a social life. And, seeing that
these things are so, how is it possible for any one to be a
man, in all the fulness of his intellectual powers, and not
make the religious confession and take the religious attitude?
It must be that the man who thinks seriously and feels profoundly is the true, the ideal man; and how is it possible
for a man to think seriously and feel profoundly concerning
the power and mystery of universal life, and that need men
have of one another which we call morality, without having
that sense of the former and that conviction of the latter
which, in their interplay and mutual support, make up the
fulness of religion? Of course, it is entirely possible for a
man to live from hand to mouth, for bread alone,— the mere
material commodity,— and so long as he has a superabun-
dance of physical comforts and freedom from all pecuniary
anxiety snap his fingers at the greatness of the mystery of
his environment and the necessity for "the fellow-heirs of
this small island life to plough and sow and reap like
brothers." But to say this is very much like saying that
a man may, if he chooses, forego the privilege of his manhood, and be a selfish epicure or sensual brute.

> "Im Ganzen, Guten, Schönen
> Resolut zu leben."

Resolved to live in beauty, goodness, *wholeness*,— that is the
mark of our high calling, that is what it means to be a real,
true, ideal man; and there are those who come nearer to
this mark on $300 a year than some who count their millions
by the double score.

There are those among us at the present time who would
assent to half of what I have just now affirmed, and dissent
from the other half. They would say "Yes" to the moral
part, and "No" to the universal. In English law, it has
been often said, the man and wife are one; and that one is

the man. So here there are those who say that religion and
morality are one, and that one is morality. But no. Morality is not religion until it is thought out, felt out, lived out
in such a fashion that it is something more than "mere
morality,"—the relation between man and man,—and has
become also and equally the relation between the soul and
that universal Power which,

> "call it what we may,
> Is yet the master-light of a'l our day,
> Is yet the fountain-light of all our seeing."

We may live in beauty and in goodness, but we do not live
in "wholeness" until we live in this. Religion in its earliest
dawn, before it was yet moralized, was exclusively this sense
of man's relation to a Power unseen, but felt in all the
wonderful and strange appearance of the world ; and to call
that religion, be it never so sublimely moral, that has nothing
of this most characteristic glow upon its face, is to use language with disloyal freedom and abuse.

But it is loyalty to facts as well as to the sanctities of
speech that makes the religious attitude and the religious
confession an absolute necessity for every man who thinks
seriously and feels profoundly concerning the deep things of
life.   Here, pressing on his mind and heart, is not only that
need men have of one another which we call morality, but
also pressing on his mind and heart are the immeasurable
power and beauty, order and bounty, of the material universe,
flowering and fruiting in the glory of the human, in golden
deeds that "pierce the night like stars, and by their mild
persistence urge men's search to vaster issues." How is it
possible for a man to be a man, and not experience in every
deeper moment, however it may be with him in the stress of
business anxiety or in pleasure's giddy whirl, that expansion
of the heart, that joyous lift, that happy confidence, that awe,
that tenderness, which, call it by whatever name you please
or by no name at all, is of the incorruptible essence of religion ? If such a thing is possible in any way, it is not in my

imagination to conceive that it is so; and I must hold that every man who is in truth a man is as much bound to be religious in religion's primal sense as he is to be moral, as he is to eat for hunger and to sleep for rest and love for love's sweet pain.

But to assert and prove so much is far and away from either proving or asserting that the public ministration of religion is a valid institution, deserving of the support and sympathy of all people of intelligence and earnest will. Men and women can be and do everything that makes for religion in its twofold power and grace in private isolation. Indeed, they must often be religiously compelled to withdraw themselves from such religious institutions as invite their sympathy and co-operation. If a man would have any religion left, the less he has to do with some of the most popular manifestations of religion at the present time, the better.

But to vulgarize religion here does not prevent its contemporaneous existence there untainted and unspoiled. Art and literature are continually vulgarized, and yet Raphael and Shakspere sit no less securely on their thrones. If the popular ministration of religion is not what it ought to be, so much the more need is there that those who cherish a lofty and serene ideal of what such ministration should be should band themselves together for its public recognition. If there are but two in any given community, then those two; if there are two score, then those two score; if there are two hundred, then those two hundred, and so on. The common recognition of religion is of the very essence of religion in its most characteristic quality. It is the symbol of men's common needs and aspirations, and therefore it demands a common recognition and a common life. The Latin proverb, *unus homo nullus homo,*— one man is no man,— has nowhere a more striking application than exactly here. Morality has never been defined more aptly than as "the art of living together." And what, then, is more natural than that men should come together for the contemplation of its generous ideals, and band themselves

together for its sure defence, unless it be that with the same
heaven above them all, the same earth beneath their feet,
the same mystery enfolding them, they should come together
to lift up a common heart of wonder, reverence, awe, and
trust, and love to the Eternal Power in whom we live and
move and have our being?

For it is not, you will notice, as if the beginning and
end of the whole matter were the attainment for one's self
of the best quality of the religious life. Granted that,
with such spiritual helps as are now generally accessible in
any solitude not hopelessly remote from the express company and mail, a man might nourish in himself a spiritual
life of noble purity; yet no man liveth to himself, and no
man dieth to himself, said the apostle, and Shakspere
echoed him across the ages,—"Spirits are not finely
touched but to fine issues."

> "God wills that in a ring
> His blessings should be sent
> From living thing to thing,
> And nowhere stayed or spent.
>
> "And every soul that takes,
> And gives not on again,
> Is so a link that breaks
> In heaven's love-made chain."

From first to last, in the course of my Brooklyn ministry,
a good many people have come to me with a kind of flat-
tery, my response to which has somehow disappointed them.
One and another has said: "I do not come to hear you any
more, because you have helped me to get along without
you. You have enabled me to go alone." I should not
speak of an experience so personal, were I not sure that
it is that of many other ministers in our Unitarian pulpits at the present time. I have but one answer to make
to all such flattering protestations: All the more reason,
then, why you should be my helper, why you should gird

yourself to spread in wider circles the truth and good to which you think you have attained. The true church no more exists exclusively for the saving of individual souls from spiritual penury than it exists for the saving of individual souls or bodies from an eternal fiery hell. It is a company of men and women less bent on the getting of some moral and spiritual benefit for themselves than bent on the doing of some moral and spiritual good to others. We are proud of the motto over our church door: "The truth shall make you free." It is a good motto. But it needs to be supplemented with another: "To do good and to communicate." The old motto is subject to a gross and miserable interpretation; namely, that, the truth once safe in our possession, we are free to go our way in selfish isolation. If you have a truth which stirs your mind, your imagination, and your heart, which quickens you to brave surrenders and to generous deeds, it is a sword upon your shoulder knighting you to join with each and every other who has been likewise called for the communication of that truth to souls that hanker for they know not what, but whom you dare believe your vision can sustain, your word can satisfy and cheer and bless. There is no discharge in this war. To enlist at all is to enlist for every march and every battle till you fall, one soldier of the many who have somewhat advanced the unconquerable hope of man.

Of course there is nothing in all this to make it clear why you, or you, or you, or anybody else, should stand by me in my particular work, should give your time and thought and money to the maintenance of this particular church. There are various tendencies at work in the community. One is a tendency to obscure and bury in emotional slush all of those intellectual aspects of the religious situation which are so evident and so important, not only to the learned scholar, but to every honest mind. Another is a tendency to exaggerate these aspects, and to identify them with the substance of religion; and hence to conclude that for this substance we have no longer any need. Another is to privately acknowl-

edge all that criticism and science have done to invalidate
the traditional formulas, but to go on using them as if nothing had happened,— as a kind of practical humbug that we
cannot get along without, or without much inconvenience.
If these tendencies were exhaustive of the religious situation,
it would be impossible to find any work for such a church as
this of ours in the religious field. But there is another tendency. It is to frankly acknowledge all that criticism and
science have done to invalidate the traditional formulas, and
at the same time to recognize that the reality, *not of these
formulas*, but of the essential dignity and glory of religion, is
in no wise impeached by such invalidation. And with this
tendency this little church of ours has been in line throughout its brief and uneventful history from 1851 till now. It
invites the sympathy and co-operation of those to whom this
tendency seems sound and sweet and good,— sounder and
sweeter and better than it could otherwise be,— because the
danger threatens more and more that the enthusiasm of
an ignorant emotionalism and the calculating selfishness of
ecclesiastical dishonesty will divide the religious world between them, and rule it according to their will. Is it not
worth while, think you, for those who are neither of this
house nor that, and who still do not believe that the reality
of religion has perished with its superstitions, to band themselves together here and there and everywhere for the maintenance of this reality? I believe it from the bottom of my
heart. You must believe it, too, or you would not be here.
But you may very well believe at the same time that this
church is not doing what it ought to do for the great principle
it represents. There, too, we are agreed. But whose the
fault? Not yours or mine, but yours *and* mine,— in what proportion it would be invidious to set forth if I could. Of this,
however, I am sure : that, if we all could bring, to serve our
purpose here, the enthusiasm and devotion which some of
you have always brought, we should enjoy a far more vigorous life than we do now. It is a purpose worthy of the
strongest manhood and the rarest womanhood that this town

affords. There is no truth it does not welcome, no science that it fears. If we could make it known to all the people of Brooklyn as it is known to us in our most serious hours, these narrow walls — no, nor the widest in the city — could not contain the company that would throng to do it honor and to sound its praise abroad.

THE BESEECHING GOD.

However it may be about our prayers to God, how is it, do you think, about God's prayers to us? You have not thought, perhaps, that there are any such prayers. But there is certainly a beautiful suggestion of them in the New Testament phrase of the apostle, "as if God did beseech you." This, also, is one of the phrases that the revisers have despoiled, so that now it reads, "as though God were entreating by us." But the old meaning is not gone; and, if it were, it would not make a particle of difference. Every good thought of the old mistranslation is just as good to-day as ever and just as much a divine revelation and a word of God, for what makes any saying or writing a divine revelation and a word of God is the beauty and the truth and the help that there is in it. That is the most inspired which is the most inspiring. This cannot be insisted on too often or too earnestly, so long as the majority persist in seeking for the signs and proofs of inspiration and revelation in some particular place or time or personality.

As if God did beseech you! The phrase as it occurs in the New Testament is but a figure of speech. It says "as if." It does not say that God *does* pray to us, that he *does* beseech us. And yet that he does actually do so is one of the most obvious things in the whole range of our experience. And while to many excellent people the wonder of the centuries has been that God has not answered their prayers, or the prayers of other people better or more religious than themselves, the real wonder all along has been that God's prayers to men have so often met with no response or with only the faintest and most superficial. Is it not so? Consider just a few of these innumerable prayers

that like a fountain rise continually from out the world's
great heart, and then find me mistaken in this strong assurance, if you can.

One of them is the habitual order of the world. Of
course, this is a circumstance which makes a different impression now from what it did in the faint red and greyish
morning of the times. Who does not know Richard
Hooker's large and sumptuous affirmation of the significance of order in the world, or, as he called it, law? "Of
law," he said, "there can be no less acknowledged than that
her seat is the bosom of God, her voice the harmony of the
world. All things in heaven and earth do her homage,—
the very least as feeling her care, and the greatest as not
exempted from her power." But there was a time when
many people were extremely disinclined to this way of thinking about law, a time when the difficulties of science were
the consolations of faith, and the victories of science were its
despair. Every field annexed to the demesne of order was
supposed to make so much narrower the range of God's
complicity in the world of matter and of man. It must be
confessed that the scientific people were often quite as foolish as the religious in this matter; for they imagined the
same foolish thing, only, where the religious were anxious
and frightened, the scientific, especially the smaller kind,
were arrogant and hilarious, and did their best to aggravate
the anxieties and fears of the religious with the assurance
that in a little time they would have a world without God.
But there could hardly be a grosser misconception than that
the order of the world, or rather the sense of this order, had
always been opposed to the feeling of God's presence in it
until very recently, when a few philosophers and poets came
to the help of an atheistical science and a trembling faith
with the assurance that more law meant more God, and that
the mysteries of law were more religious and inspiring than
the mysteries of ignorance and blind credulity had ever been.
The Old Testament abounds in praises of the orderly arrangement of the world,—"The sun knoweth his going

down," "Seed-time and harvest shall not fail," and so on.
And these orderly arrangements are cited as the proofs of
God's protecting care. New every morning and fresh every
evening are the pledges of his constant love.

But what did I mean by saying that law, or order, is one
of the prayers of the beseeching God? I meant that the
order of the world has always been an invitation and an ex-
hortation to mankind to make its life an orderly and law-
abiding thing. The ordered circumstance of life has in all
ages been an answer to this glorious prayer, whose words
are constellations, galaxies, sun, moon, and stars, the faithful seasons, gravitation, weight and measure, heat and cold.
It is the order of the material world that has initiated and
enforced the order of the human world. This has ticked
into time with that as one clock, in the fable, ticks into time
with another clock. Man in his orderly arrangements does
but "fetch his eyes up to God's style and manners of the
sky." The very secret and the end of life is the harmony
of organization and environment. The unhappy man, the
unsuccessful man, the wicked man, is simply a misfit, a round
peg in the square hole.

Now, when I said that the wonderful thing is not that
God does not answer our prayers, but that we do not answer
his, I did not mean that we do not answer his at all. To say
that would be a foolish or a wicked misrepresentation; for
the answer to God's great prayer of law and order has been
only less glorious than the prayer itself. It is as glorious as
all the manifold arrangements of our human life that are
conformed to the regularities of natural law, to the seasonal
changes, to the properties of matter, magnetism, electricity,
chemical affinity, and so on. By the known properties of
steam God prays men to make their boilers thick and strong;
by the known properties of wood and iron he prays them to
lay this way and not that their beams and rafters and the fair
courses of those gleaming stones with which they build the
habitations of their peace, the monuments and temples of
their pride.

Man, then, is not inexorable to God. He listens to that great heart-moving prayer which is syllabled in the majestic order of the world. Beholding as in a glass this order, he is changed into the same image from glory to glory, even as by the Lord, the spirit. He has his choice to do this or suffer and be broken on the wheel he will not use to turn his mill and grind his wheat and corn. The burnt child dreads the fire. Men are but children of a larger growth. They dread the various things that hurt and hinder them. They cleave to those that give them help and speed. And thus they come to find an ordered beauty in their lives. And still the wonder is that, where the voice of the divine beseeching is so sweet and strong, men do not always listen to its prayer, that they so often disobey the laws which are already known, and are so indifferent to the discovery of those which, if discovered and obeyed, would bring them an assured felicity and an abiding peace.

Another prayer of God to men is that whose words are, to a wide extent, the same words that resound in that great prayer of the divine order which is continually making its appeal to men. The words are the same; but they are differently arranged, and so the meaning is different,— beauty, and not order. It is observation and analysis that attune the ear to the beseeching of the world as it is conceived by science in the harmony of its laws and adaptations; but the apprehension of beauty is synthetic. It is a flash, a revelation. Science has beauties of its own; but neither the telescope nor the microscope has anything in its field so beautiful as that which almost every night hangs over us, the beauty of the heavens as it strikes the naked eye, nothing so beautiful as the unanalyzed woods and waters, the grasses and the flowers, the clouds that make the morning and the evening fair, and sketch on the celestial blue a beauty rarer than its own. Is it not in all these things as if God did beseech us to co-operate with him, to resolve not to be satisfied with mere passive appropriation of the original beauty of the world, but go to work to make something

beautiful with our own hands, with our own brains, with our
own shaping spirit of imagination? And to this prayer of
the Eternal, as well as to the other, the answer has been
often rich and full and grand. We call this answer art, and,
like the divine commandment, it is exceedingly broad ; for it
includes painting, architecture, sculpture, poetry, and music.
There are those who imagine that some of these are superfluous. What painting of the artist is as beautiful as the
living, breathing beauty that we know in woods and fields,
in skies and waters, in faces fair enough "to slay all a man's
hoarded prudence at a blow"? Ah! but we want the beauty
of the woods and fields to come and stay with us. We want
to be reminded of these things when we are far away from
them here in the city's loud and stunning tide of various
care and crime, to know that they will wait for us until we
come again. And, as for the beauty of fair faces, men are
not privileged to look at more than one or two in any satisfying way. I know that there are portraits, too, so personal,
so intimate, that, if we look at them too long, they seem to
look at us with injured modesty and soft reproach. And,
still, there is a difference between the painted and the real
flame. Then, too, it should be said, the painter, the sculptor, never dreams that he is making something better than
the living form or face. Only he wants to be a fellow-work-
man with God, to renew the ancient rapture of the Almighty
in the creative act ; and it must not be forgotten that there
are forms of art wherein there is, as it were, some elongation
of the Almighty's arm, something achieved which he cannot
achieve without the human help.

What is there in nature corresponding to the melodies and
harmonies of Mozart and Mendelssohn and Beethoven and
Wagner? Those who are wise in such things tell us that
not even Shelley's lark or Keats's nightingale could sing one
single chord, only a succession of notes,—these certainly
of a most rare and penetrating sweetness. And this men-
tion of Shelley and Keats reminds us that the poet's art, as
well as the musician's, is a distinct addition to the range of

natural beauty. Granted that not even Wordsworth could report half the beauty of the natural world; that no dream of fair women Tennyson might dream could equal the reality which daily walks abroad; that Shakspere's men and women have their match and shame in living Hamlets and Othellos, Portias and Cordelias. And, still, as all our sensuous perceptions of the outward universe are, as the psychologists assure us, non-resembling signs,—a truth which our own observation easily confirms,—so are the forms the poets use to express their fancy and imagination so many non-resembling signs; and one, without irreverence or impiety, may conceive the conscious God as finding a new pleasure in the creations of his poets, as, in a less degree, in a fine show of rhododendrons or chrysanthemums, such as you and I have often seen. And once they stirred my heart in such a way that I broke out into a little sonnet-song about them after this fashion : —

> O you great beauties, who can never know
>   How passing fair you are to look upon!
>   I, 'mid your glories slowly wandering on,
> And almost faint with joy that you can glow
> With hues so rich and varied, row on row,
>   A corner in my heart for him alone
>   Must keep who hath in your fair petals shown
> Such things to us as never had been so
> But for his loving patience, sweet and long;
>   Ay, and no less to the clear eye of God,
>   Who never yet in all his endless years,
> Till you out-bloomed in colors pure as song,
>   Had seen *such* fairness springing from the sod
>   As this which fills our eyes with happy tears.

Well, so it happens that God's prayer of beauty has not gone unheeded altogether,— nay, but has had a large and wide response; and yet, when we remind ourselves what a prayer it is, full of what strong entreaty, pulsing through time and space for countless centuries, the answer to it has not been — I think you will agree with me — so very gener-

ous or remarkable. To go about our city streets, to look
into our Christmas windows, is to wonder whether men do
not prefer ugliness to beauty, after all. That is, the most of
them. They go on making ugly things,—ugly houses, ugly
furniture, ugly clothes,—when they might make things beautiful and lovely with less trouble and expense.

But, you may say, all are not artists born, and very few
are made. As with the poet of the proverb, so with all the
rest. True, very true ; and what then ? Is there no answer
that those who are neither born artists nor made artists can
make to the beseeching beauty of the world ? Do not believe it.

> " I saw the beauty of the world
> Before me like a flag unfurled,—
> The splendor of the morning sky
> And all the stars in company.
> I thought, How wonderful it is !
> My soul said, There is more than this."

And there *is* more,—the beauty of the inner life. It is
true, as Milton said, that that also ought to be a true poem.
Yes, a true picture and a statue white and pure ; a temple,
too, broad-based upon the earth, but lifting up a spire like
Salisbury's into the heavenly blue ; a piece of music full of
wandering melodies, with a great harmony pervading all. It
is true that there are such lives,—that they outnumber far
the pictures and the poems, the symphonies and sonatas,
the statues and cathedrals. It would go hard with us if they
did not. And they are everywhere. " Even in a palace
life may be well led." *Even* in a palace ! It was an emperor who said it, and he said but what he knew. Even in
a hovel, too. Even in the most ordinary slices of our city
brick and stone, houses tipped up on end, like the micaceous
slate and other strata of our New England hills. So, then,
if we cannot make pictures and poems, why not do this
better thing which is possible for you and me ? As if God
did beseech you, shine the stars of heaven, and the earth
puts on her beauty ever fresh and new. Why make our

lives a blot, a stain, a smirch, on this beseeching loveliness?
Why not take up the song of Whittier, and sing,—

> " Parcel and part of all,
> I keep the festival."

And why not do more,— not merely sing as Whittier sang,
but do as Whittier did? Why not?

But time would fail me if I should endeavor to enumerate
the hundredth part of all the prayers which the beseeching
God sends up to us from out the glorious meaning and the
splendid pageant of the world. In the fore part of my sermon I spoke as if the new translation of my text, " as though
God were entreating by us, " were something less suggestive
and impressive than the former rendering, "as if God did
beseech you." But now it comes to me that the new render-
ing goes back into the old, and carries it a step beyond, or,
rather, furnishes it with a new and striking illustration.
" As though God were entreating by us." That is the significance of all the great and good who have made the
course of history beautiful and noble with their high examples and their holy trust.

> " Ever their phantoms arise before us,
> Our loftier brothers, but one in blood;
> At bed and table they lord it o'er us
> With looks of beauty and words of good."

In the traditional theology it is said that we have a medi-
ator, an intercessor, with God. That is a doctrine which
need not be examined at this present time. Meanwhile,
how many mediators, how many intercessors, God has with
us! all heavenly and mundane things, and then — immeasurable addition ! — all human things as well.

> " God's doors are men; the Pariah hind
> Admits thee to the perfect mind."

Yes, and admits the perfect mind to us. And, if the lowest,
how much more the higher and the highest in their various

degrees! This is the reason why it is so good for us to
read of saintly and heroic lives, of golden deeds, of noble
sacrifices gladly made for truth and righteousness. For if
these examples do not summon us to braver things, if the
music there is in them does not lift at our feet so that they
are weary with forbearing, and they cannot stay, but must
take the forward path, however steep and hard, then are
they verily our accusation and our shame. And here is the
inestimable advantage of such a book as the New Testament, or rather three such early pamphlets as the first three
Gospels, telling the story of the life of Jesus in such a way
that not all the integuments of the mythologists can so dis-
guise his actual proportions that we cannot see what a true
life was here, what a true poet, what a great loving heart,
what a passionate sympathy with all sorrowful and sinful
folk, what an honest hatred of self-righteousness and hypoc-
risy! It is true that the New Testament is like the sun and
air. We are so habituated to it that we take it for granted,
and we make good the wisdom of Goethe: "Words often
repeated ossify the organs of intelligence"; for with words
often read it is the same. It was a devout Episcopalian
who told me that she had put her New Testament out of
reach for a whole year, and then came back to it with a new
sense of its importance. And I know another lady who
went the round of nearly all the great religions, dabbled in
Brahminism and Buddhism, knew all about *Atma* and *Karma*
and that sort of thing, or as much as anybody, and then
woke up one morning and discovered — the New Testament,
and found it wonderfully sweet and good.

> "She had wandered on the mountains, mist bewildered;
> And, lo! a breeze came, and the veil was lifted,
> And priceless flowers, which she had trod unheeding,
> Were blowing at her feet."

I have often thought how wonderful the New Testament
and the life of Jesus would appear to us if we could come
upon them in an entirely fresh and natural way. I never

read my dear friend Samuel Johnson's sympathetic studies of Brahmanism and Buddhism and so on without wishing that he might have come to the study of Christianity just as he came to them, not tired of hearing Aristides called the Just, Jesus called perfect man and perfect God, but with unbiassed mind and heart. But all this is by the way; and I must hasten back into the main road of my discourse.

For it is not as if God's intercessors with us, by whose lips and lives he is forevermore beseeching us to make our lives some better, holier thing, were all dead and buried, all men and women of the past. They walk the earth to-day; their tender shadows fall upon us as we, lame from our birth, lie at the gate of the temple which is called Beautiful; their words encourage us; their actions shame the dull inertia and the sordid selfishness of our habitual lives.

> " Whene'er a noble deed is wrought,
> Whene'er is spoken a noble thought,
> Our hearts in glad surprise
> To higher levels rise."

And, if we do not content ourselves with "feeling good," as people say, or with feeling bad,— *i.e.*, with the luxury of self-accusation and contempt, as many do,— but straightway go about to practise some obedience to the heavenly vision, then for that time, at least, God gets an answer to his prayer: his beseeching has not been in vain.

Consider also how the happiness of a good conscience, the pains and penalties of an evil conscience, are, or should be, of such potency with us that here also it is as if God did beseech us to choose the straight and narrow and avoid the broad and crooked way. That wickedness is the pursuit of pleasure is a doctrine that from first to last gets much unfavorable comment from the course of things. The wicked people are often miserably unhappy. Perhaps the wickedest are not. It may be with them as it was with those whom Swedenborg saw, or imagined that he saw, in hell,— as happy there as were the good in heaven. Not punished, there-

fore? Nay, because "they that are in sin are also in the punishment of sin." But, however it may be with the wickedest,
with those whose conscience is not dead the way of the transgressor is hard. Truly, they make their bed in hell; and,
if God is also there, it is to stir the fire. They cannot read
of any fault akin to theirs, and not flush hot with burning
shame or feel a sudden coldness at the heart. A nobility
contrasting with their shame has much the same effect.
Hardly can they take up a novel that it does not seem
written about them, or go to see a play that does not seem as
obviously prearranged to catch their conscience as Hamlet's
was to catch the conscience of the king. Then all the
powers of the imagination league and lend themselves to
make the misery more keen. The most unsuspecting visitor
is awaited as a messenger of doom; and they are as if they
rode in spiritual nakedness, their every sin exposed, while
every key-hole had its peeping Tom, a witness of their
shame. And, then, upon the other hand there are the
visions of a pure and honest life; and they stand abashed in
their presence, and feel "how awful goodness is, and virtue
in her shape how lovely,— see and feel their loss." To
think of these things seriously — and how can we think of
them at all, and not think of them seriously and solemnly?—
is to wonder that more people, if they are not enticed into
the right way by the beauty of holiness, are not scared from
every other by those shames, regrets, and agonies which are
the portion of the man or woman who, knowing what is best,
chooses the poorer and the worst.

Once more, God makes the voice of others' pain and
misery his voice, pleading with us to remember those whom
he seems to have forgotten. Among all the golden deeds of
history, what one do we remember with more admiration
than that of Sir Philip Sidney dying on the disastrous field
of Zutphen, and foregoing the cup of cold water because another's necessity was greater than his own? There is a battle
raging which has centuries for its hours, and races for its
regiments and battalions, whose incidents are revolutions,

reformations, here the initiation of a new religion, there the emancipation of a race. And in *this* battle we are soldiers each and all; and, if sore wounded now and then and craving a cup of water for our thirst, behold some fellow-soldier hurt more cruelly, and, if we have the knightly temper, there is no other thing for us to say but, " His necessity is greater than mine," no other thing for us to do but to put the proffered cup aside. But this is not the most common situation. The most common situation is that some have all they need of water, wine, and every sweet and precious thing, and some have none of all these things; and the necessity of these is not to those as it should be,— as if God did beseech them out of their abundance and excess to give the fainting brother, be he friend or foe, that which shall stanch his wound, and, if it cannot save his life, so touch his death with human pity that he may say as one did say in a soldier's hospital at Washington, as he felt the strong embracing of the nurse's arms about him, " Underneath me are the everlasting arms."

As if God did beseech you! O friends, it is not as if his prayer to us were this or that. It is the boundless whole. It is all worlds and times, all men and things, all literature and history, all art and song, all exaltations of triumphant love, all agonies of shame and sin, all blessed memories of those who have expected us to be good and true, all tender hopes of some day meeting them again and being with them where they are. " As if God were entreating you by us." To-day, if you have heard his voice, harden not your hearts.

CHRISTIAN UNITY.

THERE has been a great deal of talk of late concerning
Christian unity; and various conferences and churches have
proposed bases of belief and form on which, it seemed to
them, all Christians might unite in cordial fellowship. The
Roman bishop whom we call the Pope,— an ugly transformation,— the Italians, very prettily, *Papa*. and the French
Le Pape, has earnestly expressed a wish that there should
be one fold and one shepherd,— his Church the fold, and he
the shepherd,— and, encouraged by the remarkable approxi-
mations which the English Church has made to the Roman
in matters of doctrine and ritual, has invited it most cordially to reunite itself with the Church from which it schis-
matically separated three centuries ago. Not to be outdone
in courtesy, the Archbishop of Canterbury, the Primate of
the English Church, answers the papal letter, and invites the
Roman Church to join the Anglican, that there may be one
fold and one shepherd,— the fold *his* Church. and *he* the
shepherd. Then, too, there have been certain Grindelwald
conferences arranging terms of mutual concession : and the
Congregationalists at their convention took a similar course.
But the scheme of unity which has been most talked about
is the famous " Lambeth Quadrilateral," by which is meant
the proposals for unity issued by the conference which met
at Lambeth, the palace of the English Primate, in 1888. It
was a conference attended by the bishops of the whole Anglican communion, and the four propositions were : —

A. The Holy Scriptures of the Old and New Testaments,
as containing all things necessary to salvation, and as being
the rule and ultimate standard of faith.

B. The Apostles' Creed as the baptismal symbol, and the

Nicene Creed as being the rule and ultimate standard of faith.

C. The two sacraments ordained by Christ himself, baptism and the Supper of the Lord, ministered with unfailing use of Christ's words of institution and of the elements ordained by him.

D. The historical episcopate locally adapted in the methods of its administration to the varying needs of the nations and peoples called of God into the unity of his church.

The term "Quadrilateral," as applied to these four propositions, is, I suppose, of military origin. In military parlance it means four mutually supporting fortresses. Now, fortresses are intended to keep other people out rather than to draw them in. And this Lambeth Quadrilateral seems to make good this military origin of its name in several particulars. It seems well adapted to keeping people out,— all those who do not believe that the Bible contains everything necessary to salvation, or that it is the ultimate standard of faith; all those who do not believe that the Nicene Creed is a sufficient statement of Christian faith, seeing that it is all theology without a syllable of ethics; all those who find nowhere in the New Testament any reason to believe that Jesus instituted either baptism or the Lord's Supper; all those who, on the one hand, question whether the Episcopal is the best form of church government, and all those, on the other hand, who want something more than an historical episcopate, even an apostolical, basing its magical efficiency on a direct descent of episcopal ordination from the twelve apostles. The Lambeth proposals were substantially the same as four propositions issued by the American House of Bishops in 1886. But at the last Episcopal Convention these same propositions were voted down by a large majority, and the cry was, "The Prayer Book from cover to cover the only door by which the heathen can come into our inheritance"; and, as the Thirty-nine Articles have not yet been "bound on the outside," as Dr. McConnell prophesies they will be soon, the cause of Christian unity, so far as the Episcopalians — its leading advocates heretofore — are concerned, seems to have had a violent set-back.

None of the schemes that I have indicated have made any overtures to people of your faith and mine. The Pope is ready to receive us, if we will acknowledge his supremacy and infallibility and all that follows in their train; the Congregationalists are willing to receive us back, if we will assent to theological propositions which hundreds of their own clergy cannot accept in any simple and straightforward manner; the Lambeth Quadrilateral encouraged our surrender with four propositions, no one of which we could accept without extensive qualifications, if at all; while the new basis of union offered by the Episcopalians, "the Prayer Book from cover to cover," invites us as the opposing guns at Balaklava invited the six hundred to their doom.

But, if we cannot accept any of the proffered hospitalities of the older churches, may they not possibly accept ours? They are very simple even in comparison with the simplicity of the Lambeth Quadrilateral: "These churches accept the religion of Jesus as love to God and man; and we cordially invite to our working fellowship any who, while differing from us in belief, are in general sympathy with our spirit and our practical aims." This is our basis of unity. It is not a quadrilateral. It is a circle whose centre is everywhere, whose circumference nowhere; whose centre is everywhere where there is honest thought and purpose, whose circumference is exclusive of no honest thought or doubt. It has worked well among ourselves. It was adopted at our Saratoga Conference in 1894 with tumult of acclaim, with trembling hearts and streaming eyes, when some that had for long years been of us, but not with us, or with us under protest without equal rights, found themselves reinstated in our fellowship as securely as they had always been established in our heart of hearts. And, not to be outdone by the Pope or the Archbishop of Canterbury or

the Congregationalist Convention or the Lambeth Conference, some of our good people at Washington offered a
resolution which, after some amendments in committee, was
passed by a unanimous vote. It was: "*Resolved*, That the
National Council give the basis of our Conference the widest
possible publication, as a sufficient basis not only for 'Christian unity,' but for the religious unity of the world."

But, should this publication be never so wide, I, for one,
should not expect to find our little kingdom suffering violence and the violent taking it by force in their sharp haste
to unite with a communion so simple in its terms of union
and so inclusive in its spirit. Its terms are too simple
for the great majority of Christian folk. Its spirit is too
inclusive. There never was an honored legend which said
less, except for its last phrase, than that which runs, "In
things necessary, unity; in things not necessary, liberty; in
all things, charity." The trouble is that we are not agreed
as to what things are necessary and what things are indifferent. The Roman Catholics think that their infallible
Church and Pope are necessary; and, consequently, if our
National Council should send our Resolution to the Vatican, it would get no favorable answer. It would probably
get none at all. Nor would the Archbishop of Canterbury
be a whit more appreciative of our extended hospitality than
the Pope; while, of course, our "love to God and love to
man" can have no attractions for those whose ideal basis
of unity is "the Prayer Book from cover to cover," and as
little for the Congregationalists, whose basis of union is substantially the creed which was exhumed a few years ago in
the old burying-ground at Plymouth, and is called "The
Burial Hill Confession." And yet I trust that there are
wandering sheep who do not love any of the folds ecclesiastical that I have named, nor the Methodist fold any better,
nor the Baptist, nor the Presbyterian, but who will be attracted to our simpler keeping and our wider range, to
whom love to God and love to man are a sufficient bond, or
who, unable to say even "God" aloud, yet find themselves

drawn to men who can. or by our open-mindedness and our evident desire to make life better worth the living for as many as we can help and cheer.

Hence you will see that the horoscope which I have cast for Christian unity is not so favorable as to commend itself to those who are particularly interested in this line of thought and work. And yet I would not be inappreciative of the good that is involved in it, while I cannot but believe that many of those who imagine themselves aspiring to Christian unity in a broad and generous way do wofully deceive themselves. Their aspiration for religious unity is at the bottom only an aspiration for the extended power and greater glory of their particular church. They are like political partisans who are ready and enthusiastic for a union ticket, a citizens' ticket, a non-partisan municipal ticket, if their party may be allowed to name the candidates and to scoop the spoils. "We Episcopalians," said Dr. Greer, of St. Bartholomew's, New York, at a meeting of some Baptist union,—"we Episcopalians have had a good deal to say lately about Christian unity ; but, if you look at us real hard, you will find out that our unity means that we want you all to believe as we do." But sometimes it means worse than that, which wouldn't be so bad; for, if men believe a thing, and find it good in the believing, comforting them in their sorrows, strengthening them in their temptations, shaming them in their sins, there is nothing shameful in their wishing all men to believe as they do, however foolish it may be for them to expect it. But sometimes this aspiration for Christian unity only means that we want other men to come and swell our crowd, whether they believe as we do or not. In the amenities of churchmanship during the last quarter-century there has been quite as much covetousness of wealth and numbers as indifference to theological dogmas or religious liberality.

And then, too, is it not quite within the bounds of possibility that in ecclesiastical matters, as in political, "harmony" may be overdone? Harmony is a good thing, but we can pay too dear for it. We may give up to party what was meant for mankind. It was certainly an interesting fact that the Lambeth Conference was willing to make its basis of unity so broad, as it was a painful one that the late Episcopal Convention narrowed it to "the Prayer Book from cover to cover." But, if men believe that "the Prayer Book from cover to cover" is the best possible basis of union, they are more to be commended if they stand resolutely by it than if, so believing, they surrender their belief for an ecclesiastical advantage. There are bishops, Anglican and American, who do not believe in the episcopate as something historical and traditional, but as something apostolical and magical; and such would not have proved themselves better men by acceding to the Lambeth statement than by opposing it. There are others to whom baptism and the Lord's Supper mean appalling mysteries : and it would be simply wicked for them to accede to the free and easy statement of the Quadrilateral. Such overtures as those of the Quadrilateral could only tend to alienate such men as these I have described, to drive them into the Roman Church. Are we quite sure that the loss for Christian unity upon this side would be made up by the gains of a few Presbyterians and Congregationalists upon the other? for this is the utmost the overtures of the Quadrilateral were likely to affect. To imagine that any Congregationalist Convention or any Presbyterian Assembly could hand over the Congregationalists or Presbyterians bodily to the Episcopalians is to imagine foolishly. They might make the formal contract, but they could not deliver the goods.

There is this also to be said : that, for the soundness and efficiency of intellectual life and moral purpose in the Christian world, it would not be a good thing for all the churches to come together on a basis of Christian unity, exclusive of all differences. Christendom is better as it is, with the infinite variety and richness of its creeds and forms, than it would be with a creed so short and simple as that of our National Conference,— "love to God and love to man."

The other churches will either make no answer to our invitation or they will say : We believe that, but also something more. And, though the something more is not so grand and high as "love to God and love to man," it is something worth standing for and living by; and we are not willing to give it up or to relegate it to any dust-hole for old lumber, any limbo of dead-and-alive beliefs and forms. Nor do I see how any Unitarian can repress a sympathetic motion of his heart when such an answer is borne back to us upon the eastern or the western wind. Take our own case. I thank Heaven that we can show better cause for our existence than the "glittering generality " or " blazing ubiquity " of our Conference preamble, whichever it may be. I grant you that that is the white light of heaven. But, as I prefer to have that light in nature broken into colors of transcendent beauty by the huge prisms of the earth and sky, so I prefer to have that light as it shines in our Conference preamble broken up into the transcendent beauty of our thoughts of God and man, and life and death, and truth and · duty. Our Western brothers found the better way. They made their welcome broad enough for all, and then they made a frank and noble statement of "things commonly believed among us." That is the kind of statement we should make. But it is of less importance that we make it in the contracted space of one or two pages published formally than that we make it with the generous amplification of our habitual speech and publication. So made, it may not only attract, but repel; but we shall at least say something that is not being said all the world over, and those that come to us will be our own.

But we should make a great mistake if we imagined that uniformity or similarity of belief is the only or the most efficient bond which can hold men together. Let communism have its way; let all the material possessions of mankind be divided among our fourteen hundred millions, share and share alike, and how long would it be before some would have twice, thrice, ten times, a hundred times, as

much as others? Not very long. And let all the believers
of the earth establish a church of universal unity on the
basis of that minimum of belief they hold in common, and
how long do you imagine it would be before the indefinite
homogeneity began to differentiate into a definite heteroge-
neity of contrasting and opposing sects? Not very long.
But what would tend to such a process quite as much as
the inability of men to think alike — so long as they haven't
all one brain and mind — would be the loyalty to things traditionally precious. Let us take a concrete illustration that
is close at hand. It is a fact beyond impeachment that the
modern Unitarian and the modern Jew, or even the most
orthodox, are much nearer together in their thought of
Jesus and their religious thought in general than the modern Unitarian and the Christian orthodox. And, if Jesus
could come back, as many have been imagining of late,
while he might feel tolerably at home in a Jewish syna-
gogue, he would be utterly dumfounded in an orthodox
Christian church. What a lot of notions of which he had
never thought or dreamed! What a jangle of words this
Nicene Creed, without a syllable of mercy or justice or any
of the weightier matters of religion! But this is by the way.
What I am driving at is this: that, because of this community of thought between the Unitarian and the Jew, it does
not follow that they should or that they can immediately
coalesce into one homogeneous religious body, as here and
there they are advised to do by well-meaning persons. And
why? Because our Unitarian tradition is not the Jewish
tradition, and traditions furnish many points of coalescence
and coherence where beliefs furnish few or none. "We do
not bear the root," said the apostle, "but the root us."
And our root is a Christian root. Therefore, we must
"abide in the vine." And the Jew must do the same. This
matter has been brought very close to me during the last
few weeks by a remarkable little book written by a sister of
that Emma Lazarus who sang the songs of her people, good
as the "Marseillaise," with such a splendid vehemence that

her heart broke in the singing, and she died. But this book by the sister is an impassioned summons to the Jew to merge himself in Christianity. Do you know that, as I read, I found myself reading as a Jew, and well-nigh the words of scornful reprobation and rejection burst from my lips: "No, no, and no a thousand times! By all the disabilities of my people in the past, by all the insults and injuries they have suffered and are suffering still, by their persecutions and expatriations, by the Ghetto's sordid hell, this people shall be my people, and their God my God. If Jesus, who was a Jewish prophet, has any higher word for me than Jeremiah or Isaiah, that will I take to heart; but it shall be as a Jew I hear, even as a Jew he speaks. A race we are not, as your anti-Semites fancy when they would excuse their wickedness; but we are a people naturally selected by two thousand years of struggle for existence, by ignominy and shame and wrath and bitterness, and a people we will remain,— if less miserably isolated than we have been, so much the better, but loyal to our tradition of unspeakable suffering and misery unto the bitter end, if bitter it must be."

So said the Jew in me in answer to the summons to her people to surrender, or to unite with Christianity, which sounds unmistakably in Josephine Lazarus's little book. And I am sure that what I said was said in order that the thoughts of many hearts might be revealed. Just after reading the book, I expected to meet my dear friend Rabbi Gottheil, and I was greatly disappointed in not doing so; for I meant to speak with him about the book, and I had lively expectations of the splendid outburst of indignant scorn with which he would repudiate its meaning and intent.

Well, if the Baptist and the Methodist, the Presbyterian and the Episcopalian, the Universalist, the Unitarian, and the Orthodox Congregationalist have no such tradition as the Jew inviting them to loyalty, each has its own tradition, abounding in great names and high examples, in stirring histories of things bravely done and borne; and it is more powerful to maintain their several autonomies than any minimum of common religious thought and feeling is or should be to compel the merging of their several autonomies in a common fellowship,—"thanks to the human heart, by which we live" far more than by any theological belief.

And yet, and yet, we must not be too easily discouraged in this matter of our vision of religious unity, which, if it means for some only more names upon their lists, for many others means something very grand and beautiful, something so grand and beautiful that the vision ought to be a prophecy and pledge of its embodiment soon or late in a divine reality in which many thousands will rejoice. The wind bloweth where it listeth, and you cannot tell whence it cometh or whither it goeth. "Even so the kingdom of heaven," Jesus said, "cometh not with observation." And with that kingdom of heaven, which is named Christian unity by some, and religious unity by others, it is much the same. It does not come by ecclesiastical management, by Grindelwald conferences, and Lambeth quadrilaterals, and such things. It comes by steadily increasing mutual understanding and religious sympathy, by admiration of the men who, in this or that body, transcend its limitations, and are acknowledged all around as worthy of all love and praise. It comes by the steadily increasing interchange of personal amenities. The ocean steamer and the summer resort are doing more to develop a very real religious unity than all the ecclesiastical conferences and politicians. The Unitarian meets the Presbyterian on the polished deck or broad piazza, and finds there is no smell of sulphur in her garments. The Presbyterian discovers that the Unitarian has neither horns nor hoofs. How many thousands, reading the sermons of Phillips Brooks, have felt their hearts leap up as much in answer to his word as if he had been of their own sect! We have a nice bit of religious unity, too inclusive to be merely Christian, at our ministers' meetings in New York. There are about as many Universalists as Unitarians, and our unity would not be more complete if the Universalists should call themselves Unitarians or *vice versa*. And there comes Rabbi

Gottheil; and no one is more welcome, though he comes frankly as a Jew, and says many things which we do not believe. If he doesn't believe that Paul wrote the Love Chapter in Corinthians, he believes it is the greatest chapter in the world; and we are quite content with that. But this sort of thing is not the exclusive privilege of our little coterie. There is something like it in hundreds and thousands of cities, towns, and villages in the United States. Everywhere the ancient barriers are broken down. My Roman Catholic friend, whom I have never seen, writes to me every week, and sometimes oftener. He, a priest, calls me his godfather in his affectionate letters; and we have much religious agreement, as when he sends me one of his little poems, like the following, called "The Cowslip," to which my heart responds : —

> " It brings my mother back to me,
> Thy frail familiar form to see,
>   Which was her homely joy.
> And strange that one so weak as thou
> Should'st lift the veil that sunders now
>   The mother and the boy!"

Innumerable the friendships and the courtesies that unite in one humanity the members of the most widely separated sects. In the smaller places the cordial interchange of sympathies increases at a more rapid pace than in the cities, where the question, "Who is my neighbor?" is one that thousands cannot answer right. In the smaller places ministers of the different churches, whose pulpits fifty years ago would have shrivelled like a snake-skin and cast out a preacher not accredited as Baptist or Methodist, and so on, as the case might be, now make exchanges without even causing popular surprise, and their people, who fifty years ago were segregated from each other in gloomy and suspicious isolation, now have to stop and think whether so and so is true blue or not; or, if they know, they hardly care. And then there is the unifying element of scientific thought. It is not here or there, but everywhere,—an atmosphere which people must breathe if they breathe at all. And to breathe it is to acquire a certain movement of the blood and brain, which makes all who feel it of one mind and heart to a very great extent. I am sure that we are tending to a more inclusive unity of intellectual perception and belief, and I expect the time will come when there will be a wonderful agreement among all the churches as to all the important things; but, when it comes, I hope and trust that we shall not have one all-including Church, but pretty much the churches that we have now, each loyal to its own traditions of nobility and saintliness, devotion to principle, enthusiasm for truth and righteousness, but willing and glad to have its priests and prophets free to come and go, hearing in their own tongue in which they were born the speech of many lands. Even now, of such Christian and religious unity we have no mean development. It has grown fast of late, and it will grow and grow until its tide of generous sympathies shall catch up and sweep along the most unwilling minds and the most selfish hearts.

There are great unifying forces working in our time. Science is one, and literature is another. When a hundred thousand people read the same great book with glowing heart, they are worshipping together quite as beautifully, their religious unity is quite as perfect, as if they should all come together, and recite the Apostles' or the Nicene Creed in unison. And literature, for all its aberrations, is making for the one thing that was more characteristic of Jesus than any other,— sympathy with human misery, a passionate desire to lift up the hands that hang down and confirm the feeble knees. It is making equally for intellectual sincerity and for the subordination of the letter which killeth to the spirit that maketh alive. Another unifying force is common work. "The communion of saints!" Did it ever occur to you that the meaning of "communion," the root signification of the word, is "common work"? And such communion is one of the most unifying things under the big sky. The Abolitionists never called themselves "the Anti-slavery

Church." But what a true Church of God they were!—assimilating to themselves their own from all the churches, and welding them into a unity compact as the primeval granite against the onset of the slave power, North and South. Our partisan politics are divisive in these days. Like Martin Luther for his theses, here we stand for protection or commercial freedom; and, so help us God, we can no otherwise. And we are no worse for that so long as we allow to every man the right to think as he must think, which we claim for ourselves. And, so far as I can make out, there are just as good men and just as intelligent and thoughtful men for free silver or bimetallism as for the one metal, and that gold.* But there are other things concerning which all honest, earnest, and right-minded men must think alike,— the reform of our municipal administration, the purging of our civil service, municipal, state, and national, from those elements of personal and party greed which demoralize it and disgrace it, and make it a by-word and a hissing among men. Here are two kinds of work, closely allied no doubt, in which good men of every church and sect can join with mutual sympathy and trust, and the Romanist cannot say to the Protestant, "I have no need of thee," nor the Unitarian to the Presbyterian, "I have no need of thee"; for they all need each other, and the good causes need them all for their prosperity. There are other causes that I have not named in which also good men of every communion and opinion can unite, the promotion of temperance, and the organization of charity, so that it shall not pauperize three or four for every one it helps. But I am keeping you too long. I trust that I have said enough to make it plain that, if there is much in the planning and scheming for Christian unity that does not appeal to us as sound and good, and that is sure to come to nothing, there are within our reach the possibilities of a Christian and religious unity that is very real and true, and large and fair, and excellent and grand. Nay, more: it is not wholly in the future tense. Its kingdom is at hand.

* But not so many of them, I sincerely hope and believe.

The forces of civilization and sympathy, of literature and science, of common social work for generous and lofty ends, have already built it up into a form and comeliness which are not by any means to be despised,—

> "A temple neither pagod, mosque, nor church,
> But loftier, simpler, always open-doored
> To every breath from heaven; and Truth and Peace
> And Love and Justice come and dwell therein."

And why not we with them?

PEACE AND WAR.

PEACE on earth, good will to men! How can we but be glad that such a sentiment, worthy of being sung by angel choirs, was rescued from oblivion and set in the forefront of the gospel history! A sentiment so pure and high might well be the salvation of any legend in which it is imbedded. And who shall say that it has not been the sentiment that has preserved the legend rather than the legend that has preserved the sentiment? But, whether it has been so or not, the sentiment has been preserved; and, though it did not prove prophetic of any sudden change in the habits of communities or individuals, and though not even yet does the world's international life embody its ideal force and beauty, I dare believe that by the music of this angel song the hearts of men have been allured to gentler ways than they would else have known, that there would have been still less peace on the earth, and still less good will to men, if the Christian world for nineteen centuries had not been confronted and rebuked by this ideal, however unattained as yet, however unattainable for centuries to come.

Peace on the earth! Does it look much like it in the newspapers, magazines, and official papers of the day, in the war budgets of the different nations? Does it look much like it in Armenia, where the antipathies of race and of religion have engendered feuds of an infernal bitterness and barbarity, whose daily incidents are as indiscriminate slaughters as have ever marked man's inhumanity to man? Does it look much like it when all the European powers are menacing the Turk, and could, if they would, compose " the sick man " to an everlasting sleep by a mere *fiat* of their collective will, but, should they do it, would probably proceed at once to tear

each other in pieces over his emaciated corpse? Does it
look like it in France, with one laughing eye on her new-
stolen Madagascar, and the other, ever sleepless, on her
German frontier, biding her time to stab her hated conqueror
in the back or fling her gauntlet in his face? Does it look
like it in the Far East, where the collapse of China in her
conflict with Japan has made a carcass of her for the vulture
eyes of Russia and the other powers? Does it look like it
in Germany, where the young emperor, a miserable anachro-
nism, a feudal overlord in modern clothes, is always clamóring
for more money, for more soldiers, when already his gigantic
military system is an intolerable vampire, sucking away the
strength of Germany's young manhood, the vitals of her industrial prosperity? Does it look much like it in England,
doubling her naval armament and the appropriations for her
army in a hardly less degree? Does it look much like it in
America, where the voice of an irresponsible and reckless
press is still for war, with whom or for what it matters precious little, so that there be war, where legislators who do not
deliberate are industriously occupied in promoting international feuds, where the Congressional chaplain, with a
sharp eye to windward where consulships and such things
await a change of administration, in the name of one who
has been called the Prince of Peace, prays thus with the war-
dogs: "May we be quick to resent anything like an insult
to our nation! . . . So may thy kingdom come, and thy will be
done on earth as it is in heaven." Peace on earth! Does
it look much like it when the President of the United States
sends to our Congress a message which contemplates the
awful possibility of war between the United States and Great
Britain, and representatives and senators tread upon each
other in their wild haste to stampede the House and Senate
and the country into a rush of blind and stupid acquies-
cence?

Fifty years ago the peace societies were flourishing.
They do not flourish now. Then Charles Sumner gave the
great oration of his manly youth, "The True Grandeur of

Nations"; and many there were who believed on him, though
the great, thieving expedition into Mexico was already well
begun. Would as many now believe on a young man
of whatever splendid parts, whatever wonderful nobility of
face and form, whatever voice of deep-toned melody, who
should come believing such things as Charles Sumner believed in 1845, and saying such things as he said? I doubt
it very much. I am not sure that good men should desire
to have it so. "In our age," he said, "there can be no
peace that is not honorable, there can be no war that is not
dishonorable." Could he himself say this in 1861, when the
war for union and emancipation had actually begun? Lowell
had been with him in 1845; but in 1861 he recognized that
"the sheathed blade may rust with darker sin," and sang,—

> "God give us peace, not such as lulls to sleep,
> But sword on thigh and brow with purpose knit;
> And let our ship of state to anchor sweep,
> Her ports all up, her battle-lanterns lit,
> And her leashed thunders gathering for their leap."

Without shedding of blood, there was no remission. Peaceable emancipation would not have cost one-third as much,
to say nothing of the loss of life and joy and the long entail
of social misery and crime. But peaceable emancipation
was impossible. The South did not wish to sell her "divine
institution" for mere sordid gold. And so there *had to be*
another war; and there may *have to be* another yet,— ay,
many more down the dark future.

But meantime it is unquestionable that to be "first in
peace" is unsatisfactory to a great many people at the
present time. I am speaking now without any reference
to immediate events. Various factors have contributed to
this state of mind. For one thing, a good many have
stopped short in the first pages of the history of social
evolution; and, because war was formerly a divinity that
rough-hewed the ends of social justice, they assume that
it must be looked to for the shaping of them to the finest

issues of the present and all coming time. Such would do
well to notice that Spencer, the first of evolutionists, is the
most inflexible antagonist of the military spirit now alive.
Another factor, and a far more general one, in our fighting
temper is the increase of our national strength, and with it
the increased consciousness thereof. Here, too, men learn
by halves, remembering that it is excellent to have a giant's
strength, but tyrannous to use it like a giant. Another
factor in this temper is the hope of gain which feeds upon
the recollection of the splendid fortunes that were made by
the army contractors of the war, the nation's torn and bloody
plumage but an opportunity to feather their own nests.
But the principal factor in our altered temper is the idealization of war in the abstract in the light of our own great
contest and our own glorious victory. If you want to see
the ruddiest flower of this idealization that has bloomed
upon our soil, you must get a late number of the *Harvard
Graduates' Magazine*, and read Judge Oliver Wendell
Holmes's Harvard Memorial address upon "The Soldier's
Faith.".* It is, as he interprets it, faith in the divine beauty
and eternal necessity of war. "Some teacher of the kind,"
he says, "we all need. In this snug, over-safe corner of the
world we need it, that we may realize that our dull routine
is no eternal necessity of things, but merely a little space of
calm in the midst of the tempestuous, untamed streaming of
the world, and in order that we may be ready for danger."
To have shared "the incommunicable experience of war" is,
he tells us, "to have felt, to still feel, the passion of life to
its top." Given that, and the soldier is content,— content
even to be forgotten in his grave.

> " And, when the wind in the tree-tops roared,
> The soldier asked from the deep, dark grave,
> 'Did the banner flutter then?'
> 'Not so, my hero,' the wind replied:
> 'The fight is done, but the banner won.
> Thy comrades of old have borne it hence,—

---

* A personal letter from Judge Holmes regrets the coincidence of its publication with
the present hue and cry.

Have borne it in triumph hence.'
Then the soldier spoke from the deep, dark grave,
'I am content.'"

"Then he heareth the lovers laughing pass;
And the soldier asks once more,
'Are these not the voices of them that love,—
That love,—and remember me?'
'Not so, my hero,' the lovers say:
'We are those that remember not;
For the spring has come, and the earth has smiled,
And the dead must be forgot.'
Then the soldier spoke from the deep, dark grave,
'I am content.'"

Thank God, *our* soldiers are not forgotten, and are in no danger of being forgotten, even if they were content to have it so, counting themselves of all men the most fortunate to have died for their country in her hour of sorest need!

It may be that such a passionate idealization of war as that of Judge Holmes is necessary for the instruction of those people who can see only one side of war,—the awful sacrifice of life. No, that is not the word for it: the sacrifice, *the voluntary sacrifice*, is just exactly what they do *not* see. They see men killing one another. They do not see *the being killed*, the *gladly being killed*, in some great cause. But those are few who have this optical defect. With most people it is just the other way. What makes the literature of war so fascinating to us all is the splendid courage it displays. I almost broke my heart the other day reading a story in which there was a dead soldier lying across the breast of his companion as tragically as Cordelia on the breast of Lear. It was a story of the Franco-Prussian war, and that was one of the most wicked wars that ever choked the course of history with its stream of blood. And the young man had no business to be there, for he was neither French or German; but that didn't make his courage any less. That courage fascinates us all. It is that which draws the boy to his Henty book, the grown man to his "Napier" or "Grant." Sometimes, I am bound to say, the killing part is at the fore. It was often so with Robert Louis Stevenson, his reeking shambles burying his native genius out of sight. But, in general, the terrible beauty of war in literature and in the popular imagination is in the "good courages" which it involves. These bulk the vision of the ardent youth or man. They see this side intensely, and they see no other.

And be it far from me to dim by one mis-spoken word the shining of this splendor in your hearts. But let us look at it as eagles at the sun; and is there anything in the history of our own memorable conflict and its subsequent results that should make war *as such* seem any more desirable to us, any less to be avoided, shunned, and hated than if there had been no Grant or Sherman, no Gettysburg or Shiloh?

We must not forget the splendid courage nor the willing sacrifice. No, we must not. But, then, no more should we forget the horrible details of slaughter, wounds, and death. the shattered limbs, the lacerated flesh, the hospital's slow, weary, wasting agony, and homesick tears in the long watches of the nights that would not tell, the broken lives, the broken hearts and homes. And there are other things which we must not forget. You know, perhaps, the German proverb that every war leaves behind it an army of heroes, an army of cripples, and an army of thieves; and we have had them all. Alas! how many of the heroes under ground, how many of the cripples wishing they had shared their fate! Can we deny the thieves? Is that too harsh a name for the great swarm of human vultures who fattened on our vitals, when we were bound, Prometheus-like, upon our frosty Caucasus? for those who, when the war was over, must find new fields for the rapacity which its sordid opportunities had nourished, forever crying, like the daughters of the vampire, "Give, give!" coming down on the administration of Grant,— too generous and unsuspicious for his place,— and capturing it by a more subtle strategy than he had encountered on the embattled field? Another obvious legacy of the conflict was the inflation of all business methods, all standards of prosperity. The modest gains of former times no longer satisfied. Luxury was henceforth the habit of the rich, lavish expenditure the habit of the poor. And then a great war costs so much money, and the expense goes on long after the time when the war-drums throb no longer and the battle flags are furled. Ours costs us every year of late some two hundred and fifty million dollars. The most of it is, no doubt, well spent; but what a drain upon our industrial energies, what a bias on our questions of revenue and taxation! No reasons here for not going to war again to-morrow, *if that is the right thing for us to do*, but reasons manifold and impressive why we should not go to war if we can abstain from it with honor, why we should not think war a good thing in itself one whit more than we did forty years ago. The vast demoralization of our currency, which to-day hampers our business prosperity, is nothing but one hateful legacy which has come down to us from the artifices to which we were compelled to resort under the stress of war to meet the swelling flood of national liability. These are not merely economical considerations, and, as such, too trivial or sordid to be considered for a moment, when a great crisis thunders at our doors. They are intensely moral. They enter into the every-day morality of every citizen of the United States. They are not beneath contempt, nor even beneath the serious consideration of any man or woman who is trying to think what is true and right and best about the business which is now uppermost in all our thoughts. They prove, I think, that, in despite of our inexpugnable consciousness of the necessity and righteousness and crowning good of our great civil conflict, so far is that experience from making war *as such* any more beautiful or desirable than it did before, it makes it more hateful than ever, more than ever something to be avoided, if it can be avoided, as the very gate of hell.

What President Cleveland said is true, "There is no calamity which a great nation can invite which equals that which follows a supine submission to wrong and injustice, and the consequent loss of national self-respect and honor, beneath which are shielded and defended a people's safety and greatness." But between "supine submission" and war's dread alternative there be many stations at which, without the slightest loss of self-respect and honor, we may arrest our steps. Nor can I doubt, I must not, will not doubt, that we shall pause at one of these. If we do not, whichever party to the strife is most to blame, the event will be such a disgrace to the civilization of our century as it has not heretofore sustained; and woe be to that nation at whose door shall lie the folly and the sin of plunging England and America into fratricidal war!

In certain press despatches printed on Friday last, and which in almost every paragraph ran blood, like Cæsar at the base of Pompey's statue, it was not without a pleasant shock of difference and surprise that I came upon the following words: "Men who have seen war, and remember some of the miseries and the train of expenses and excesses following war-conditions, deplore the fighting talk, and counsel the wise discretion that will enable us to avoid a conflict." Does that sound to any of you very un-American, very unpatriotic? It sounds to me as sweet and good as if Washington were speaking, or Lincoln or John Bright or Richard Cobden or Tom Hughes, all equal friends and lovers of America. It indicates, I think, the position which we all should take and hold, until to hold it longer is impossible. The general and quite satisfactory assumption is that war is sure to come. Such an assumption is all the easier now because it has been the assumption all along of a great multitude of noisy ranters, whenever there has been a difference with England or Spain or Chili or any other country. But heretofore it has not come, in spite of the assumption and the noisy rant, in spite of thousands of editorials and speeches admirably calculated to bring about a war, if there was any excuse for one whatever.

The force of public opinion is immense; and in such times as these every man should see to it, if possible, that he

counts one in the formation of that opinion. He should endeavor to understand the merits of the case; and until he
does understand them pretty well, or thinks he does, he
should not put on his war-paint and shatter the firmament
with his battle yell. How many of those who are most vociferous for "the honor of the nation" have taken the
trouble, do you imagine, to inform themselves what the
Monroe doctrine is, or have given to the despatches of Mr.
Olney and Lord Salisbury the six or seven hours it takes to
read them carefully? Not one in a thousand. Not one in
a dozen of the Congressmen who were for rushing through
the indorsement of the President's message without send-
ing it to committee. And every self-respecting man in the
community should resent the endeavor of the thoughtless
and passionate majority to drag the questioning and dis-
passionate minority at their chariot wheels. In the annals
of American journalism I have seen nothing more contemptible than the attempt to brand as mean and cowardly and unpatriotic any tendency to deprecate haste, or to question the
soundness of the President's position, or to deplore the needless threat with which he brought his message to an end.
"It is above all things necessary," we are assured, "that the
President should seem to have our undivided and unqualified support." Then it is above all things necessary for us
to tell an abominable lie, for nothing is clearer than that he
has not our undivided and unqualified support. Leave out
of the account the partisan opposition, which reflects merely
a comic fear that this business may inure to his advantage,
and there are many of our most learned jurists, our most
distinguished civilians, our most thoughtful publicists, our
most substantial business men, and among these as loyal
friends as Mr. Cleveland has ever had, who profoundly question the soundness of his position, and regret unspeakably
the tone of his message, as better calculated to aggravate
existing difficulties than to make them less. And it is above
all things necessary that at this painful juncture these "men
of light and leading" should get in their word. Of igno-

rant acclamation there is sure to be enough. So, too, of
cowardly subserviency to what seems to be the ruling spirit
of the hour. But, if there are any people who have a steady
pulse, a level head, a talent for deliberation, we should
attend to them as best we can.

But there are other things I deprecate as much as ignorant acclamation ; and one of these is the ungenerous and, I
must believe, unjust imputation to the President of unworthy
motives,— motives of political ambition,— in short, of an attempt to rehabilitate the waning fortunes of his party, and
perhaps his own, by means of the popularity accruing from
the assumption of a warlike attitude in behalf of Venezuela.
I have respected him and honored him too long, too earnestly, to pay a moment's heed to such a railing accusation,
even when it is voiced most definitely and loudly in the
house of those who have been hitherto the most loyal of his
friends. To think such things of him, I should have to
think of him as one who would have to take his place in history lower than the lowest of his predecessors,— lower than
Johnson, lower than Buchanan, lower than Polk or Tyler.
The man who could put our national peace in jeopardy in
furtherance of his personal ambition or a partisan success
would be a moral monster ; and the man who should indulge
in big war talk to " tickle the ears of the groundlings," with
a mental reservation in favor of a quiet backing down a few
months hence, would be a man for whom no suit of motley
could be sufficiently absurd. I dismiss as utterly unworthy
of a moment's deliberate assent such an impeachment of
Mr. Cleveland's honor or intellectual sobriety ; and, if any
of you have given it shelter in your bosoms, I beg that you
will cast it out as if it were some loathsome thing.

But it is quite another matter to conceive that Mr. Cleveland has succumbed at last to the imperious stress of that
public sentiment which has been clamoring all along for " a
vigorous foreign policy," and which has been fertile of denunciation of the President as un-American, unpatriotic,
indifferent to the recognition of America as a great world

power, and so on, *ad infinitum* and *ad nauseam*. He is a man of morbid sensibility; and it has chafed and fretted him beyond endurance to have his patriotism and national pride impeached, until, at last, it is as if he had said to those of his own party and those of the opposition who have been hounding him on to some warlike demonstration, "The villany you teach me I will execute; and it shall go hard but I will better the instruction." And one of the compensations which I anticipate for the innumerable ills that will be sure to flow, and are already flowing, from the present posture of events, is a very general retirement of those editors and politicians who have been dancing the war-dance of late with so much mutual admiration. They have been so noisy that their numerical strength has been greatly overrated. They have stirred their witches' cauldron with great glee, and now on their affrighted eyes dawn the dark shapes of what their words would mean when written large and red in the concrete of action. It would be safe to prophesy that, when things have settled down again, we shall hear a great deal less about "a vigorous foreign policy" and "manifest destiny" and universal annexation than we have been hearing for some years past.

But I am speaking quite too much as if I understood the merits of this controversy,—a thing which as a layman in such matters it would be presumptuous for me to pretend. But I have done my best to understand them, and much that I have said already is unwarrantable and absurd except as it harks back to my persuasion that the refusal of Great Britain to accept our arbitration was not unnatural after the receipt of Mr. Olney's letter of July 13. The tone of that letter was, to my thinking, clearly the tone of prejudgment, although it was elaborately iterative of our freedom from all bias. Hardly can I conceive of a letter less adapted to the end it had in view, yet no one can wish more heartily than I that our arbitration had been accepted. Notwithstanding the prejudgment that inhered in Mr. Olney's letter I think our arbitration would have been entirely just. Heretofore our relation to the matter has been largely *ex-parte;* for Venezuela, the plaintiff, has been our client, and Great Britain, the defendant, has been at little pains to put her case in our hands. But with the responsibility that a formal arbitration would have entailed, with all the facts and arguments in our possession, and with the best judicial mind our country can afford brought to bear upon them, I am quite sure we should have arrived at a just decision.

As to the merits of the controversy, the fact that we have just voted $100,000 for a commission to decide upon them makes it absurd for any private individual to speak confidently of them. It would appear that, at the cession of British Guiana by Holland to Great Britain in 1814, the boundary line between that province and Venezuela was quite indeterminate. It became a matter of controversy in 1844, and has remained one ever since, except when the Venezuelans have been too busy cutting each other's throats to give it any thought. Read Mr. Olney's letter, and you will be convinced that the course of England has been a course of irregular aggression; that the boundary of her colony has swept back and forth, like the waves of a tide upon a beach,— more forth than back. But read Lord Salisbury's despatches also, and you may not feel so sure of that. The retreating boundary from time to time has, he assures us, been a gracious concession to the Venezuelans of what Great Britain had always claimed as hers by right. But the matter is full of uncertainty; and I should think it would take our commission from now until the election of — his name does not occur to me — next November, to work it out. Meantime it is the height of the ridiculous for any one to dogmatize about it, or to get angry with any one who is not prepared to say exactly where the line should be.

But, if Mr. Olney's letter had ended with the history of the controversy and a plea for the allowance of our impartial arbitration, it would, I cannot but believe, have been much more efficient than it has proved to be in its entirety. Thomas Benton once complained that somebody had in-

jected a stump speech into the belly of a certain bill, and
Mr. Olney has certainly injected a stump speech into his
letter. Its second half reads much more like an old-fash-
ioned Fourth of July oration than like a grave and cautious
diplomatic paper. This part is an exposition of the Monroe
doctrine and its application to the case in hand. In advance
of the present stage of this controversy, some one, with a
touch of humor in a serious discussion, said that the Monroe
doctrine had "no more to do with it than with the damna-
tion of non-elect infants." That is a liberal phrase, but it is
hardly an exaggeration of the fact. I am giving you my own
impression, but not without the happy consciousness that I
am one of many in this view, and that some of the many
are persons of the greatest weight. The Monroe doctrine
was announced by President Monroe in his message of
Dec. 2, 1823. It had two leading positions: 1. "That our
Western continents are not henceforth to be considered as
subjects for future colonization by any European powers."
We have Mr. Olney's assurance that position does not concern us now. 2. "We could not view any interposition for
the purpose of oppressing [the free and independent States
of this hemisphere] or controlling in any other manner their
destiny, by any European power, in any other light than as
the manifestation of an unfriendly disposition toward the
United States." So cordial was the sympathy of England
with this doctrine that it was published by her advice; and
Charles Sumner contended that it should be called the Canning doctrine rather than the Monroe doctrine, Canning
being in 1823 the king's prime minister. It was inspired by
the character and conduct of the Holy Alliance,— Russia,
Prussia, Austria, and France,— which, violently reacting
from the French Revolution, was trying everywhere to force
its absolutist principles and governments upon the world.
Those principles have nowhere now, except in Russia, any-
one so poor as to do them reverence. It was against the
attempt of the Holy Alliance "to extend its system" to our

 Not necessarily entailing a retaliatory war.

hemisphere — a very real danger in 1823, when we were a young nation of nine million people — that the Monroe doctrine was declared. But will any one outside a lunatic asylum maintain that Great Britain is attempting to impose the despotic system of the Holy Alliance, which she repudiated even in 1823 as earnestly as we, or any system of her own, despotic or monarchical, on Venezuela? Will any one maintain that we have less political sympathy with Great Britain than with a characteristic Spanish-American state, whose inhabitants have been busy for nearly twenty years out of the last fifty cutting each other's throats?

Is it not agreed to-day that the British system is practically more democratic than our own,* seeing that they could abolish their monarchy to-morrow by act of Parliament, while we could not lengthen the term of our President's office without a constitutional amendment adopted by Congress and by two-thirds of all the States? The Monroe doctrine opposed the extension of European despotism to this country as "dangerous to our peace and safety." Does any one imagine, with England already owning half the hemisphere, our neighbor from the Atlantic to the Pacific, and as good a neighbor as could be desired, that the acquisition of a few thousand square miles of territory in South America would be "dangerous to our peace and safety"? To answer this question in the affirmative would be humiliating in the extreme for a nation of seventy million people.†

Here is the sum and substance of the Monroe doctrine : We should consider the attempt of any European *despotism* to impose its system on a free American State as dangerous to our peace and safety. Is Great Britain a European *despotism*, and is she trying to impose her *despotic system* on any free American State in a manner that is dangerous to our free institutions? If not, the present controversy does not

* See Sir Henry Sumner Maine's " Popular Government."

† What *would* endanger our peace and comfort, if not our safety, would be a war that would find Canada as friendly as need be, and leave her as unfriendly as possible. Such, at any rate, was the result of the northern campaigns of 1776-77 in the Revolutionary War.

come within the scope of the Monroe doctrine. The matter
in dispute is a boundary which apparently has never been
clearly defined, and therefore leaves either side free "to
claim everything" within certain extreme limits. It is a
monstrous shame and pity that the dispute should not be
amicably settled.

That the action of our government will conduce to such
a happy consummation we have little reason to believe.
There was no need of any threat of war. It has encouraged
evil passions abroad and at home. It has already been the
ruin of much honest business; and will be of a great deal
more. Our national currency, already in a precarious condition, is put in a much graver plight. But let us hope for
better things. The political opposition will see to it, above
all things, that no advantage inures to the President or his
party from the course of events; and therein we have one
powerful brake upon the flying wheels. Then, too, it may
be that the finding of our commission will be favorable to
Great Britain; and, if it should be so, the only thunder of the
war-cloud will be the crack of a tremendous joke, the expense of which we shall share with Venezuela. If the finding tends the other way, as not improbably it may, we shall
not, I trust, tender it to England as our ultimatum at the
cannon's mouth, but with so much gravity and serenity and
good humor that, if she does not accede to it, she will feel
obliged to show us most convincingly that we are in the
wrong. There are a thousand noble artifices which we must
exhaust before, in a cause so complicated and obscure, we
make the dread appeal that will involve us in an awful conflict with that people to whom we are allied as with no other
by ties of blood and history and literature and the heritage
of glorious names, and to whom, with us, have been committed in trust the largest promise and the dearest hope of
human life on earth.

The final outcome of our trouble will depend upon the
thought and feeling of innumerable men and women; and
what I have tried to do this morning has been to contribute

something to the justice of your minds, something to the goodness of your hearts, so that your individual contributions to the common stock of better thought and feeling may be compacted of the things that make for peace.

> " My song save this is little worth :
>   I lay the weary pen aside,
> And wish you health and joy and mirth
>   As fits the solemn Christmas-tide.
> As fits the happy Christmas birth,
>   Be this, good friends, our carol still,—
> Be peace on earth, be peace on earth,
>   To men of gentle will! "

THE LIFE-LONG JOY.

IT is hardly too much to say that the Bible has been more highly valued in the past and to this present time for what it does not than for what it does contain, for what men have put into it and taken out again rather than for what is actually there, for the mistakes of its translators rather than for the truer meanings they have missed. This state of things has been only natural, if not unavoidable, so prone are men to seek and find their own opinions in any scripture to which they go for an infallible rule, and so difficult is it for the mind of one age to enter into and interpret simply and exactly that of another far remote. The "New English Dictionary" teaches a lesson which theologians have been very slow to learn : that the meaning of words is a continual flux, and that to treat them as if they were signs indicating fixed quantities of meaning is absurd. Do our best, and there will remain hundreds of words, ideas, thoughts, in the Old Testament and New that we can never understand, their meaning is so relative to the total intellectual, and moral outlook of the ancient world. There is much that we have recovered that is so relative to changed conditions that it has no value for us, save as a record of entirely obsolete ideas ; and, with regard to much that we have not yet re-covered, and may never, we may console ourselves with the reflection that, once recovered, it would have no word of counsel or encouragement for our present difficulties, doubts, and fears. At the same time there are other sentences and passages in the Old Testament and New that roll up the ages like a scroll, fill up as 'twere the gap of centuries between our time and that of the prophets and apostles, and bring us face to face with them, heart answering to heart. It is not that these sentences and passages are, as we say, written out of time and space. It is that they are written as with the life-blood of humanity, whose ruddy color does not fade from age to age. These are the best the Bible has to give,— better, even, than the inspired mistakes of the translators which have such lodgment in the affections of the world that they can never be displaced.

One of these sentences of imperishable beauty and significance is that in the great ninetieth Psalm,— "Oh, satisfy us early with thy mercy, that we may rejoice and be glad all our days."

Simple as is the text, it contains, you will observe, an implication and an argument of which the major premise is suppressed ; namely, that, if we are early satisfied with the goodness of the Eternal, we shall rejoice and be glad all our days. It is not absolutely true. There is many a life which has a brave beginning, lacking nothing of external comfort or advantage, or of intellectual and moral help and cheer, which, as the day wears on, sees clouds arising on its fair horizons, — clouds that roll up the sky, big, not with mercy, but with trouble, grief, and pain, making a ruin of its love and joy. This happens frequently, unless life is very different now from what it was in the far times men measured by Olympiads, when the danger of being too happy so impressed them that they conceived the doctrine of Nemesis,— the doctrine of a grudging Fate, that, just when men were perfect in their happiness, would come like a strong wind, and beat upon their house and bring it to the ground. Quite opposite, moreover, to the Psalmist's implication is that lament of Dante in his immortal song, which Tennyson had made his own by conscious reproduction, when he sang —

" For a sorrow's crown of sorrow is remembering happier things."

If this is true, then was the Psalmist quite mistaken in his thought ? Such are the contingencies of life, such the dangers that attend our happiness, so many are the doors by which it slips away, that, the less we have of it, the better, if Dante's thought and Tennyson's echo of it are a true report. If they are so, the Buddhist and the Stoic way of wanting little which it would be hard to lose or miss is the way of the blessed life. But I, for one, do not believe that their report is true in any large and spiritual way. The memory of mere outward wealth, comfort, ease, and luxury, or of mere worldly position, influence, and reputation, may be a crown of sorrow for the man whose whole life has been made up of these external things ; but, for those who have resources of the mind and heart, no memory of the mere trappings and encumbrances of life which they have had and lost can be to them the hardest sorrow. I grant that, when the loss is not of these poor outward things, but of some visible presence that is dear to us beyond the possibilities of speech to tell, in the first agony of our bereavement our sorrow gets the keenest edge of its heart-piercing pain from the remembered goodness, sweetness, tenderness, of loved companionship that we have lost ; but if, as time goes on, and we enter into spiritual relations with our dead, I know, you know, we would not spare one moment of remembered joy. And, if the recollection of our lost happiness is indeed a crown of sorrow, it is no crown of thorns wounding our aching brows or wreathing them with subtle mockery, but a crown of rejoicing that such blessed things *were* ours,— a royal crown, whose high nobility compels us to all best and holiest things.

The early satisfactions which make through all the years of our maturity and age for gladness and rejoicing are not by any means coincident with the outward things that most men are striving for as if they were the only things worth having. There is a hint of this in the biographies of famous men. How uninteresting to read about are the early years of the thinkers, poets, statesmen, inventors, musicians, scholars, and reformers who were born and reared in every circumstance of luxury ! How trippingly the biographer passes over such men's childhood, knowing that he can no

more make it interesting for us than the painter can a picture of children richly dressed amidst luxurious surroundings !
A fashion-plate is quite as good.   But it is different with
the childish years that were inured to hardship and denial.
These are the biographer's opportunity.   How he likes to
dwell — and we with him — on the frugality and stern simplicity of Emerson's boyhood, on the one coat that he and a
little brother wore on alternate days, the off days going cold !
It is "the bobbin-boy," "the rail-splitter," or "the mill boy of
the slashes," who is a good magnet to draw the political enthusiasm of men who, being human, have in them the love of
poetry and adventure and romance.   And these predilections
are not confined to literature.   In men's own lives, what is
looked back upon with gladness and rejoicing is not the luxury and surfeit of its earliest years,— no, but the hardship
and frugality, the scanty clothing and the simple food, the
bed in the unplastered room, the frozen breath upon the
sheet, the sifting snow across the floor, the few books,
the fewer toys ; and, though they would not willingly subject
their children to a like ordeal, they feel that they are losing
something which nothing can quite take the place of in the
retrospect of the full-grown man.   Even if some should insist that the real source of pleasure is the contrast of the
later comfort and success with the frugality and hardship of
the early time,— which I do not believe, or only as a very
partial explanation,— even then it would appear that, to fully
enjoy the foreground of our comfort and success, it must
have a background of hardship and frugality.

How then ?   Are we arriving at the amusing paradox that
the early satisfactions which we should desire for others and
be grateful for in our own lives are not the things we have,
but the things that we have not,— the deprivations and denials
of our childhood and our youth ?   So it would seem, and yet
it is not so.   The real blessing, mercy, satisfaction, is not in
the having or the lack of merely outward things, but in the
consciousness that the true sources of life and happiness are
deeper than all these ; and, if we cannot learn the lesson

otherwise than by going to the school of hardship and misfortune, then we had better go to that school. Whether in
literature or in our personal experience, the satisfying mercy
is not the having or the lack of merely outward things, but
the fulness of life, as such, so great that it can dispense with
much that some account essential good. It is the tenderness and love, the beautiful fidelity which no wealth can
give, no hardship take away. Satisfied with such mercy, we
shall rejoice and be glad all our days in fond remembrance
of that early satisfaction. That is a miserable philosophy of
life which finds in each succeeding period only a preparation
for and stepping-stone towards the next. "I do everything," said Francis Wayland, "as if there were no next";
and that was better than to make every part of life merely
preparatory, and so rob the whole of its significance. But
memory is so large a factor in our lives — and, as we grow
older, the memories of childhood and of youth enter so much
more largely into our inner life — that, for the happiness of
later manhood and of age, there is no better surety than a
fountain of memory welling up from childhood full and pure
and sweet, no better preparation for whatever comes in
any after time than to be early satisfied with the Eternal
Goodness as it shows itself in the goodness of fathers and
mothers, and brothers and sisters, and kinsfolk and teachers
and friends. Life may be hard and dry in after years, a
desert blowing blinding sand ; but to have that memory of
early satisfaction is to have an oasis always near at hand
where one can stand up to his knees in cool water, a garden
of refreshment into which the weary mind may draw apart,
and rest itself from every curse and care.

But I am speaking quite too much as if the mercies of
our youth, whose sweet returns gladden the later years, were
all that we receive. Indeed, it is not so. In fact, there is
no fount of bitterness that works its way through all the
ledge and soil of that country intermediate between our
childhood or our youth and our maturity, and breaks forth
when least expected, proffering its poisoned chalice to our

lips, that is to be compared with a remembered goodness which we grieved and wronged with wayward wish and will. The sweet obedience and thoughtful care with which the growing boy or girl seeks to repay the mother's anxious love, the father's patient care, are treasures incorruptible laid up for them in the heaven of all future recollection. What wealth and honor would the grown man not sometimes give, what admiration and obsequious following the successful woman, if with them they could buy forgetfulness of things of which no others know,— thoughtless or cruel words spoken long years ago, selfish pursuit of their own happiness at the cost of pain (of foolish pain, perhaps) to loving hearts. I do not mean that our maturity has no sources of intolerable regret in the various relations of the home, in the parent's failure to appreciate the child's mistake, or to take the proper measure of his fault in the hot anger loosed and the injustice done at such too memorable times. Saddest of all sad pictures is that at Byron's Newstead Abbey, a picture of Lord Arundel,

> "Who struck in heat the child he loved so well,"

and such a blow that the child's reason flickered and went out. The picture shows the father in the act, and the child's vacant eyes are piteous prophecies of the evil wrought.

> "Methinks the woe that made that father stand
> Baring his dumb remorse to future days
> Was woe than Byron's woe more tragic far."

Oh, but it does not need such tragedy as that,— it does not even need the hasty blow : the cruel word is sometimes quite enough to hang a picture where the eye turned inward sees it every day, not without agony ! Happy the man or woman who, either as parent or as child, has dashed upon the mind's interior walls no pictures of his baser self with hasty, cruel hand ! Thrice happy they who, looking on the dear Madonna painted there, *their* holy mother, see in the eyes no

look of sad reproach, and read upon the lips no quivering of
unrequited trust or injured love!

But there are other aspects of my theme which I must
hasten to report. The tendency, especially of our American
life, is to postpone so long the pleasures of existence that
when at length it is men's time, as they conceive, to build
or travel, to read good books and to enjoy the beautiful
things of art, their strength is weakness and their appetite
is dull. The house is a mere vestibule to the tomb, the travel
is a weariness. Experiences that should have furnished
years of gladness and rejoicing, gone over hand in hand
with memory, are so long delayed that there is neither time
for any afterglow nor the capacity for any rich and full immediate enjoyment. Visible surroundings that should grow
familiar by long happy use, and gather sweetness of associa-
tion from a thousand joys and hopes and fears, from friendly
faces and from children's play, are postponed until in life's
brief remainder it is impossible for the new places ever to
be anything but new and strange. Nothing is sadder than
the immense disqualification of many persons of great
wealth or ample means for the enjoyment of those things
which these can easily procure. They have time for travel,
and the money, too: but they have not the preparation, without which travel is a mere Barmecide feast of splendid
dishes empty of all pleasant food. I do not think that Mr.
Henry James exaggerates the misery of the wealthy American gentleman abroad, dragged around by his wife and
daughters to see things he does not care to see, hear things
he does not care to hear, taking more pleasure in his furtive
glances at the "Stock Market" in the New York *Herald*
than in any lake or mountain scenery or any glories of
architecture or painting that Europe has to show.

If there is any sight more tragical than this, it is the man
who has retired from business without the tastes which alone
can prevent leisure from being an intolerable bore. He has
a library, of course. If he has sought the advice of a judi-
cious bookseller or friend, it has good books in it by dozens

and by scores; but, alas! he has never contracted a liking
for good books. He likes the poor ones better, and the vain
surmises and the idle gossip of the daily paper best of all.
He may have pictures, too, and good ones, if he has stuck
close to the famous names or availed himself of some tal-
ented and honest connoisseur; but, as for his enjoyment of
them, in a moment of desperate frankness he will let you
know that it is very little, or he will tell you of their fabu-
lous cost, and retail to you the dislocated phrases he has
gathered from the talk of those more confident than he, if
not better qualified to judge of " values " and " technique "
and "chiaroscuro," and so on. And if it so happens, as it
often does, that such a man with all his limitations has been
simple and sincere, he will shortly sicken of his leisure as of
tasteless food. He will relish more the crumbs that fall from
the tables of his money-changing friends than the whole
feast of his leisured opportunity. He will long for the adventures of business as Ulysses for the adventures of the
sea; and, when he can restrain himself no longer, he will
set out again in search of them, and, if he does not wreck
the fortune he has built and rigged for steady winds upon
some unknown coast of random speculation, he will do better than some others whom we all have known.

Mind you, I do not say that such an order, or disorder,
of experience as I have described is predicable of men of
wealth, as such. I do not even say it is the rule, not the exception, though, if judgment were demanded of me on this
head, I think I should incline to this decision. Enough
that it is all too common, that their name is legion whose
experience answers to the experience I have described, as
face answereth to face in water. And where it is quite
otherwise than so, where the man of wealth or ample means
brings to the leisure he has earned the ability to appreciate
and to enjoy it, the love of good books and the knowledge
what they are, delight in art and some discrimination between the noble and the trivial, the sincere and the artificial,
the love of natural beauty, the aptitude for social help, it is

where he has not put off his culture in these things until he
has the leisure to enjoy them. It is where in some high way
he has built his life after the pattern we have seen this
morning in the mount of the great Psalmist's vision of life's
natural sequence: " Oh, satisfy us early with thy mercy, that
we may rejoice and be glad all our days ! "

Just at this point I seem to feel a kind of protest coming
back to me from those whom I address, quite general,
though not equally from all,— a protest against my estimation of a business life, as if that had no mercy in it, no
goodness, that we should desire it, as if the mere heaping up
of money were its beginning, middle, end. If I have made
any such impression, the protest is entirely just ; and I bow
to kiss the rod of your displeasure with a humble mind.
But I hold to no such estimation of a business life. How
frequently have I contended that a man's business, his calling wherein he is called, is his one great opportunity for
doing good and establishing his right to be here on the
planet, getting his share of sunshine and sweet rain and all
the other beautiful and blessed things life has to give ! Yes,
and I have insisted that no munificence of social help or
charity can justify a business that is not fundamentally beneficent, or make up for the lack of justice, sympathy, and
generosity in the management of one's manufactory or trade.
Besides all this, I recognize that the mere money-getting is
to many business men the smallest part of it. They care
more for "the rigor of the game " than for the stakes. They
like to link their judgment and their powers with other men,
as rival stags their horns upon the cliffs in terrible encounters. Nay, 'tis no trial of brute strength or mere endurance,
but a trial of foresight and intelligence ; and victory in this
splendid game brings with it the joy and satisfaction of the
chess-player's " Mate ! " a hundred or a thousand fold. But,
when due allowance has been made for all these things,
there remain things of the mind, things of the imagination,
things that bring the individual into large, vital sympathies
with the great currents of humanity, its stumblings and its

fallings on the way to truth and holiness and God. There remain revelations of God in nature, history, and art, without some share in which no life is even tolerably complete, no life is anything but marred and spoiled,—the merest fragment of its possible reality of truth and good.

There is this also to be said : that, although to some men it is given to keep up in business, like a Gladstone or a Metternich in politics, the strain of unabated energy even till past their fourscore years, while still their labor is not sorrow, it oftener happens that there remaineth a rest for the people of Mammon, a time of slackening strength and will, a period of reaction from the violence of the earlier storm and stress; and that, when this time arrives, it must go hard with those who have not laid up for themselves treasures in heaven,—treasures of thought and taste, the love of nature and the love of art and books, the aptitude for public spirit and for social help. And those who would lay up for themselves these incorruptible riches must begin betimes. Hardly can they begin too soon. In middle life it is too late. The passions and the tastes that are to dominate the later life must be established in our youth or early prime. Even if it were safe to wait till life becomes "more solemn and serene when noon is past," who that is wise would have the splendor of his prime untouched by all that makes for ideality in our mortal life ? "Oh, satisfy us early with thy mercy, that we may rejoice and be glad all our days ! "

And now, if you have followed the later drift of my discourse, you will perceive that it has been in quite a different direction from the former part. There my insistence was that all our earlier years should be as full as we can fill them with all sweet and noble satisfactions,— having, doing, and being,— to the end that in all the after time we may find in them a place of blessed recollection,— books of remembrance, which we cannot open save at some pleasant picture or delightful poem or tender story of the times forever gone away. But life is not all memory, and there is better reason far than this for taking on our lips the Psalmist's prayer.

It is — and this has been the later drift of my discourse—
that not only our memory, but our life,— the meaning and
the purpose of it, the energy and passion of it,— will be
according to the manner of our early satisfactions, be they
with things unworthy of our admiration or desire or things
that have in them the making of a man. It is no absolute
rule. There are men who are made glad according to the
years in which they have done evil. Some influence of
health and healing wrestles with them in the darkness of
their self-contempt, and will not let them go until they have
received its blessing. Let us be glad there are such insur-
rections of the better life in men. But, surely, it were
a foolish thing, so far as we have in these matters any
measure of control, to squander half of life upon the chance
that something higher than ourselves may seize upon the
other half with irresistible, redeeming power. No! All of
life is not too much for high and noble things. What we
want is to rejoice and be glad all our days ; and, that we
may do so and be so, we cannot begin too soon to satisfy
ourselves with the mercy of God, the goodness of the Almighty that is extended to us, that is pressed upon us, in all
the various ordering of our lives,— in the affections of the
hearth and home, in the fidelities of our habitual tasks, in
the beauty of the external world, in the great wonders of
the painter's and the sculptor's and the builder's glorious
arts, in the illimitable wealth of thought to which so many
have brought all the patience of their toilsome years, in
the not less illimitable wealth of character that the saints
and heroes and the faithful workers of all ages have
funded for our use. Not only to the God that is above us,
but to the God that is in us, let us direct our prayer ; and to
that God let our importunity be such that, like the man of
the parable crying for bread at midnight, it cannot, will not,
be denied.

I know that many of us have left so far behind their morning visions that, whatever of sad or joyful illustration we may
find of these things in our lives, they cannot be to us an in-

spiration. For better or for worse, we have already made our choice. But there are those near and dear to us whose hearts are singing still the song of youth,—

"All before us lies the way."

And some of these, perhaps, may find some meaning in my words. Some of us may try to bring it home to them with strong appeal; and all of us, in one way or another, can make ourselves ministers of the eternal goodness to some little child or boy or girl or youth or maid, and, if we may not satisfy them with that mercy which shall rejoice and gladden them all their days, add to their stock something which in both memory and character shall work for blessing and for peace. If we can do but little, let us not on that account withhold our hand. The whole round world is made of atoms that no eye can see. Take rather on your lips and to your hearts this music of a rude and strange and yet most wondrous singer in the choir of God : —

" If I can stop one heart from breaking,
I shall not live in vain.
If I can ease one life from aching
Or cool one pain
Or help one fainting robin
Into his nest again,
I shall not live in vain."

THE NEW SINAI.

I HAVE read to you this morning the story of the transfiguration, as it appears in the Gospel according to Luke; and
I was strongly tempted to read you the same story as it appears in Matthew and Mark, just for the sake of a little incidental lesson in New Testament criticism. In the story,
as I read it, you will remember that it was the overshadowing cloud that caused the fear of the disciples. But in Matthew it is the voice proceeding out of the cloud that causes
their alarm; while in Mark it is neither the cloud nor the
voice, but the apparitions of Moses and Elias. It is a matter
of no practical importance, but it affords an interesting comment on the doctrine of Biblical infallibility and a more interesting one on the mutual relations of the Gospels. It is
evident from these differences that no one of them slavishly
copied another of the three, and quite as evident that they
were not all derived from a single primitive writing. There
are scores of such discrepancies between the first three Gospels (the fourth is one grand discrepancy with all three of
them together), and they point unmistakably to a variety of
documents back of the Gospels or to a variable oral tradition. Where the Gospels are best agreed among themselves, there is most likelihood of contact with the earliest
tradition and with the actual facts concerning Jesus' life and
teachings. It is interesting to observe that within the range
of their agreement there is no miraculous birth or definite
resurrection, and that the number and portentousness of the
miracles is very much reduced. Sometimes we can see the
legend growing, as it were, before our eyes. Thus in one
Gospel, as originally written, we have no details of the resurrection and no ascension whatever; in another, a visionary

appearance after death ; in a third, the resurrection followed by a physical ascension on the same day; next, and strangely enough by the same writer in Acts, a period of forty days elapses between the resurrection and ascension. How can the superstitious blame the rational thinker for preferring the least exorbitant of these accounts or even for imagining that the legend had stages antecedent to those which have survived in the New Testament? And how can any one who is not wholly blind to the significance of these considerations presume to dogmatize upon the strength of any word ascribed to Jesus or any event associated with his name? For this negative conclusion has been established, if nothing else,— that we can have no perfect certainty concerning anything that Jesus said or did.

So much for my incidental lesson in New Testament criticism ; and now I come back to the story of the transfiguration and to the particular text whioh I have chosen as the starting-point of my discourse. " They feared when they entered into the cloud." I have no present care as to what actually happened in that far-off time to give rise to such a story. This is the harder to make out because the working of our minds in many ways is different from that of people living then. Nor have I any present care to make out which reading is the best, that of Matthew, which makes the voice out of the cloud the fearful thing, or that of Mark, which makes it the apparition of Moses and Elias, or that of Luke, who says it was the overshadowing cloud. I take the last because it is the one I want for my immediate purpose. For life has its overshadowing clouds ; and, when they gather in about us, fear is the natural emotion of our hearts. Sometimes, indeed, we cannot fear too much. There is the cloud of sorrow, so enshrouding us that some dear friend, it may be "a nearer one still and a dearer one yet than all others," is no longer visible to us. We grope for him in the darkness, but we cannot find the hand whose strength supported us in many difficult and trying hours. What do we fear? Not that some harm has come to the loved one, nor so much, either, that in the boundless heavens, "where the skyey road-ways part," we may not find the one that leads to his embrace; but whether we shall find our life worth living with so much that helped to make it so taken away from us; whether, unshared, the daily burdens will not press us down and crush us with their weight; whether we can solve alone the painful questions that are sure to rise in every soul that is confronted with life's awful mystery. And, sometimes, alas! the fearful heart finds, as the days go by, it has not feared too much; while there are others who are a wonder to themselves, where so much has been taken so much still abides; so much the recollected goodness, wisdom, cheerfulness, avail to lift up the hands that hang down and confirm the feeble knees.

And, then, there is the cloud of business anxiety. There are many in these times who have had sore experience of this. What smiling faces have concealed from us what tragedies of sleepless nights and days of miserable futility and hopeless gloom! If the strong man had only himself to care for, he would snap his fingers in the face of fortune. But there are those to whom he has given bonds of service and protection, whom he has spoiled perhaps for hardship with his soft indulgence; and there are the good causes he would so gladly help, and the old strugglers to whom he would extend no empty hand. My observation may have been at fault; but, so far as it has extended, the impression I have got in these hard times has been one of brave endurance, of quiet heroism, under the grinding pressure of those terrible anxieties which the commercial situation has entailed. We often speak of the industrial age as if it had no opportunities for heroism equal to those afforded by the military age, of which, with monstrous unreality, we speak as something past and gone. And, certainly, its opportunities are different; but I have sometimes thought that they demand a firmer courage and a nerve of stronger iron. As between sudden death within the foeman's lines and fortune's utter wreck, how many, think you, would not choose the former as the better part? But how many have borne the latter quietly, doing their best to keep the cloud enwrapping them from chilling other hearts! And I have not lived for thirty years upon a shore where the great waves of business prosperity alternate rise and fall, without learning well enough that with loss of money there is often gain of character,— that, as between prosperity and adversity, the former, quite as often as the latter, is too heavy to be borne. I have seen men whose self-respect was so implicated in their bonds and mortgages that, losing these, the other also went; and I have seen those who with increasing wealth have come to measure all things by a gold standard, their only question henceforth what their investment will pay, be it in railroads or electrics or politics or marriage or religion! And be-tween such diversities of moral wreck there is not much to choose. A man's *life* is not in the abundance of the things that he possesses ; and not a few, both in the possession of material wealth and in the loss of it, have found that this is so.

And now I pass to the particular application of my text, which is to me peculiarly impressive. "I was born free," said the apostle ; and many of us here could doubt-less say as much. I mean that we have never had to undergo the anxiety and strain which are inseparable from the transition from the traditional faith of Christendom, intensely realized, to the free mind of science and the order of ideas and beliefs which goes along with this. But this transition is immensely characteristic of the present time ; and I have seen too much of the sufferings which it entails to wonder that anybody should be smitten through and through with fear when the cloud of intellectual doubt first broods with overshadowing wing over their minds, dim-ming the outlines of those traditional dogmas which have always been so firm and hard, and at the same time revealing, like a phantom ship seen through the mist of dawn, the ghostly mystery of the new order of beliefs, lowering porten-tous, vague, obscure, "a grief without a pang, void, dark, and drear," for some, for others meaning poignant misery.

For it is not in these things, you will notice, as if, over against the old in all its horrible deformity or selective and engaging charm, the new were seen in all its fair proportions, beautiful, complete. Abraham in the story, going forth he knew not whither, was a prototype of many who have left behind them some Chaldean Ur of long-established creed, and gone forth seeking a city that hath foundations, whose builder and maker is God. It is a cloud into which they enter, not into clear, bright sunlight, making all things sharply visible and showing them divinely fair. I remember well enough how it was with me — forgive the personal confession — when such a cloud enveloped the conception of supernatural Christianity, which before then had been about as definite in its outline as a dry-goods box or a picture frame or any other purely mechanical object. If I could then have seen the natural conception of Christianity,— I will not say rounded and complete,— but as I see it now or even as I came to see it in a few years, it would have been a very different matter. But I was granted no such vision. What I saw was that certain things which I had believed to be true were not true; but the new things that should come and fill the void which these would make by their departure,— these I could not clearly see. Something of this sort, as I go on, I seem to have told you once before ; but I am so far in that it will be less trouble now to cross the stream than to turn back. At last there came a time big with the possibilities of grave mischance. I had read Francis W. Newman's "Phases of Faith"; and now the question came, should I read Strauss's Life of Jesus which I had borrowed from my friend Samuel Johnson, enriched with hundreds of notes that he had made, crowding the margins and the fly-leaves of the three volumes. I seemed to know that, if I read that book, my tottering faith in supernatural Christianity would fall ; and that was by no means what my selfish heart desired. And thereupon the devil came to me, arrayed as an angel of light, and suggested that I should go over and see Dr. Noyes, and get his advice. I knew perfectly well what he would say,— that Strauss was not milk for theological babes, but meat for strong men, and that I must tarry in Jericho until my critical faculty had grown before settling down to such a book as Strauss. I knew that he would say something like that, and that was why I was going to ask him for his advice. I set out on my errand, and soon reached his door. But I did not go in. I walked up and down in the clear moonlight for some time ; and then I struck off toward Arlington and Lexington, along the road the British took on the night of April 18, 1775. It meant defeat for them, but it meant victory for me. For, walking miles and miles, when I got back to Cambridge, it was much too late to call on Dr. Noyes, even if I had cared to do so. To "consult my pillow" seemed the wiser course ; and I did that, going to sleep at last, and waking in the morning and settling down to Strauss for six weeks of good hard reading, which, if they left me

> " Wandering between two worlds, one dead,
> The other powerless to be born,"

made it impossible for me ever to build again the house of my traditional belief. In course of time my joy and satisfaction in my new order of belief became incomparably greater than they had ever been in what had passed away. I often wonder how it would have been if I had been obliged to pass at once from my snug and cosey supernatural-ism to the wide spaciousness of scientific thought. As it was, the Transcendentalism of Theodore Parker invited me, a cheerful half-way house, vouchsafing every man his private revelation of God, immortality, and the moral law. Then came a time when, reading Mill and Spencer much, again there came a cloud and overshadowed me ; and again I feared when I entered into the cloud. And well I might ; for, again, it was not as if I could see the coming things in their completeness set over against the things in which I had rejoiced, and shaming them with a diviner beauty. The cloud that overshadowed me made all the former things un-

certain, vague, intangible : it hid the others almost wholly
from my view. Again, like Abraham, I went forth, not knowing whither. But of one thing I was resolved,— that, if I continued to wait on my ministry,— a matter as to which I had
many painful doubts and grave misgivings,— however meagre
the message might be, it should be well within the boun-
daries of my own personal conviction. It was ; and, to my
increasing satisfaction and delight, it was not so very meagre,
after all. Once and for all I found how many inspirations,
sanctions, and defences of the moral life are safe against all
shocks of theological or philosophic or scientific scepticism
or dogmatic opposition. If at that time all that I now perceive to be implied in science as applied to the great problems of religion had been apparent to my mind, it would
have been an easy matter to burn all my ships, and take up
my home in the new country to whose coasts I had arrived.
How glad I am that grace was given me to burn them, all
the same, albeit confronted with a mountain wall that hid
from me the pleasant lands which I have since explored !

For the individual any time may prove to be a time of
theological transition. And, when this arrives, happy are
they who do not find their moral life involved to some extent in the same cloud that winds their intellectual appre-
hensions in its baffling folds. Morality may be independent
of theology ; but, when a moral system has been long associated with a particular system of theology, it is inevitable
that with the decay and ruin of the latter there should be
some danger threatening the former for at least a time.
Frances Power Cobbe has told us in her autobiography how
it was with her at the time when her orthodox belief col-
lapsed. She had been doing right, or imagined she had
been, because the Bible or Jesus had issued this or that
command, or because the hope of heaven and the fear of
hell had encouraged her to right action and deterred her
from wrong-doing. But with a human Bible and a human
Jesus and the old hell " dismissed with costs," the old motives and sanctions disappeared ; and, their place not being

supplied at once by others equally impressive, she found herself sliding down in all her feelings and conduct from the high levels of which she had been secure under the old régime. Profoundly conscious of her deterioration and profoundly miserable in that consciousness, she found herself one day out under the open sky; and *clear as that* there came a voice in her own breast, asking the question, "Can I not rise once more, conquer my faults, and live up to my own idea of what is right and good, so that, even if there be no life after death, I may yet deserve my own respect here and now, and, if there be a righteous God, he must approve me?" And she goes on to tell us how, from that hour, all things were made new for her; the tides of faith and prayer that had ebbed away began to swell again and moisten the dry places of her heart. But there was nothing very strange in her experience. It has been that of thousands entering into that cloudy atmosphere, that dim, half light in which old beliefs grow vague and insubstantial, and the new loom more as things of terror and affright than as the tabernacles of the righteous or the city of the living God. For men so tried there are two principles which have been beaten out into true swords of the spirit by the experience of many generations. One is, Pretend to believe nothing which you do not believe. The other is, Live by the truth you know, however meagre it may seem. As if divining his own future, his own temptation, and his own glorious victory, Stopford Brooke wrote in his Life of Robertson: "It is an awful moment when the soul begins to find that the props on which it blindly·rested are many of them rotten. . . . I know but one way in which a man can come forth from this agony scathless: it is by holding fast to those things which are certain still. In the darkest hour through which a human soul can pass, whatever else is doubtful, this at least is certain: if there be no God and no future state, even then it is better to be generous than selfish, better to be true than false, better to be brave than a coward. Blessed beyond all earthly blessedness is the man who, in the tempestuous darkness of the soul, has dared to hold fast to these realities. I appeal," he says, "to the recollection of any man who has passed through that agony and stood upon the rock at last with a faith and hope and trust no longer traditional, but his own."

For the individual, I have said, any time may be a time of theological transition. And this is true ; but it is not less true that our own time is one of general change,— a time when many hundreds and thousands are finding it impos-sible to accept any longer the creeds and doctrines and so-lutions to which they have assented heretofore with more or less deliberate attention. A criticism of the Bible which has revealed its natural history, which has made it impos-sible for any scholar at once well instructed and perfectly sincere to attribute a supernatural character to its various parts or an authority over and above that of its intrinsic force and charm,— this criticism for the upper millstone, and for the lower the Darwinian development of species by nat-ural selection, and not by special creation, as before,— be-tween these two the traditional belief of a great multitude of people has been ground to powder ; and, while some of these have easily adjusted themselves to the new order,— as if they had been "not unclothed, but clothed upon," and have not missed "the raiment warm by faith contrived against our nakedness,"— with many it has been quite otherwise than so, and these, it must frankly be confessed, have not been the least intelligent or thoughtful among those concerned, but frequently the more intelligent and thoughtful. It has often been the purblind and the superficial who have leaped at once to some plausible reconciliation of the results of science and the demands of the religious life ; while those of closer observation and of deeper thought, while accept-ing the results of science with a courageous heart, have mournfully confessed that they cannot find in them anything sincerely corresponding with the great thoughts of God and immortality and the divine authority of the moral law. In truth, a cloud, a huge, portentous cloud, has come and overshadowed the religious life of these,—a cloud generated by the great mountain summits of the scientific range and gradually enveloping that other mountain on which heretofore our human life has been transfigured in the light of faith and hope.

In the mean time the traditionalists, the apologists, are pointing with great satisfaction to this state of things. They are asking: "What did we tell you? Didn't we say that science had no message for the soul?" They did, indeed, thus making an appeal to coward hearts, imagining that fear of entering the cloud would keep men on the plain, content with worship of tradition's golden calf. It *has* kept many there: and many others have found the bosom of the overshadowing cloud so cold, so numbing to their sense, that they have made haste to get away from it, and back to the old comfortable haunts.

But there are those — and they are many in our time — for whom such things are impossible. There are some things from which they cannot get away. Kuenen and his fellow-critics have destroyed the supernatural basis for religion. Darwin and his fellow-scientists have substituted organic evolution for special creation in the production of all animal structures, from the moneron to man. Granted that science builds again no unity of religious thought which answers to the needs of the religious life, the despair of science does not mean the rehabilitation of the traditional belief. That has been irretrievably dishonored by the plain discoveries of critical investigation. Thank God — or, if there be no God, thank *them* — that there are men made of such stuff that they cannot be scared by any blank negation, or by such constructions as the great scientists have sometimes urged, into the reacceptance of beliefs which they know, if they know anything, are proved unsound.

> " Is this a voice, as was the voice
>   Whose speaking told abroad,
>   When thunder pealed and mountain reeled,
>   The ancient truth of God?

Ah, not the Voice : 'tis but the cloud,
    The outer darkness dense
Where image none, nor e'er was seen
    Similitude of sense.
'Tis but the cloudy darkness dense
    That wrapt the mount around ;
While in amaze the people stays
    To hear the coming sound."

And now to make the cloud more dense, while promising
the dissipation of its bewildering gloom, there comes one
after another to assure us that science and reason are not
the trusty guides we have imagined them. Here it is Mr.
Kidd assuring us that we must have some ultra-rational
sanction for the social spirit, but leaving us very much in
doubt how or where we are to get it ; and here it is Mr. Balfour supporting the claims of an irrational authority for two
reasons : first, that the fundamental concepts of science are
as inscrutable as those of theology ; and, second, that, log-
ically carried out, a demented (*i.e.*, mindless) materialism
would land us in some very disagreeable, not to say horrible, practical conclusions. These " Down with reason ! "
prophets have been received, as we should naturally expect,
with tumult of acclaim by those high in places of ecclesiastical preferment. It was exactly what we should expect that
Bishop Potter, from applauding Mr. Kidd's performance,
should sink back into his episcopal chair to sign the famous
Pastoral Letter. Undoubtedly, the advice of Kidd and Balfour and their kind will be economized to an extent far in
excess of what those who offer it would feel justified in deliberately accepting for themselves or recommending to their
friends. They have merely said, " Make to yourselves
friends of the Mammon of irrationality, that, when you fail,
they may receive you into their habitations " ; and one cannot
but question whether they have not already doubted the wisdom of their course when there comes back to them from
the purlieus of traditionalism and conventionalism and apol-
ogetics the sound of many voices, crying, " The villainy you

teach us we will execute; and it shall go hard, but we will better the instruction."

But whatever multitudes may find in such brilliant aberrations as those of Kidd and Balfour permission to go on worshipping in a temple that has been condemned as untrustworthy by a consensus of those competent in such matters, it is a certain thing that not a few will much prefer "the bitter heroism of science," if it must needs be that, to any wilful abjuration of that mighty Scientific Spirit which for a thousand years was left well-nigh without a witness on the earth, but which now for three centuries has been adding countless increments of knowledge, power, and use, and happiness to man's estate, creating for him a new heaven and a new earth, and making all things new,— among these the traditional theology. For this, as now conceived by the most orthodox, except where an incorrigible ignorance prevails, is something very different from what it was even a century or half a century ago. And, lo! we have this interesting spectacle: Orthodoxy on a monument frowning at Science for her heartless creed, when her own creed, but for the transformation which Science has wrought on it, would be a thousand times more heartless than the creed of Science in its most negative form, or the most positive unloveliness that the Calvinistic science of Professor Huxley was able to conceive. It is Science which has damped down the fires of hell and despoiled the Almighty of those attributes which an English Churchman tells us made him "the most horrible being it is possible for the imagination to conceive." It is only Orthodoxy *as transformed by Science* that has any beauty that the kind-hearted and the merciful should desire it for their own. If one had to choose between Orthodoxy as it was before the mystery of Science began working in its hideous bulk and Science in its most negative statement or its most painful implications, the man would be a fiend who would not choose the Science ten to one. For, surely, it were better to be "without God in the world" than to be in the world with such a God as Calvin's ambushed in the dark. Better to be without any hope of the immortal life than to believe in such a future as that which has satisfied and delighted the theological imagination until the most recent times.

But let me say just here that, while I am obliged to think that both Kidd and Balfour and some others of their kind have altogether missed the true significance of certain facts of our experience, we are under obligations to them for their attention to these facts, because others will now attend to them, and resolve them into some more adequate generalization than that of the great English commoner and the brilliant pamphleteer. What one of these is driving at with his irrational authority, and the other with his ultra-rational religion, is a kind of social rationality inherent in the race, wiser, *at least for social purposes*, than the reasoning of any individual person. It is Emerson's doctrine —

> " All are needed by each one ;
> Nothing is fair or good alone"—

exemplified upon the social plane. Here is something not ultra-rational, as Kidd would say, but compounded of the rationality, good, bad, indifferent, of all the countless millions of mankind. Here is something not independent of experience, as Mr. Balfour thinks, but something compounded of the experiences of all those who have at any time encountered the bright appearance of the outward universe and the mystery of its indwelling life.

And hence it is that those have much to justify them who hesitate to adopt this or that negative construction of science, this or that pessimistic interpretation of it, as a finality setting aside the Supreme Power, which, being one, men have called by many names, or that Blessed Hope which has persisted in despite of its intolerable associations, or that divine authority of the Moral Law, without which the moral life of man could never have the dignity and glory which it has had heretofore for the great ethical leaders of the race. For you will notice that, for the most part, what is called scientific negation or pessimistic science is not so much science as some

hesitation of Science to dogmatize where as yet she does not
know, or some daring generalization based upon what may
be insufficient scientific data. Theology has been growing
for I do not know how many thousand years, and certainly
it has not yet attained the fulness of its stature. Science
was later born, and what could be done for a long time was
done to stunt its growth; and yet you will find the theologians
continually speaking of Science as if it were in possession of
its maturest powers and had already spoken its last word.
Nothing could be more absurd than this. Under what pon-
derous hammers theologians and moralists have crushed
Darwin's hypothesis of the development of the moral sense!
Of course, it was imperfect, insufficient, unsatisfactory. It
was bound to be, for it was the first attempt to work out
a moral theory on the basis of organic evolution; and first
attempts are always the simplest possible, and *therefore*, generally, the most inadequate. This is one instance out of
many that might easily be named. And they all carry the
same lesson; namely, that neither the scientists nor the theologians must be in haste to accept this or that negation or
pessimistic inference of science as a finality, and as such
subversive of the rough affirmations of that social rationality
which is compact of the reason and experience of the human
race, and not, I think, without some clear reflection of that
infinite rationality of God, which is forever immanent in all
the working of the natural and human world.

Here is no call for any one to accept for himself conclusions which he is obliged to think irrational nor for any one
to withhold what he conceives to be the fair result of scientific thought. We cannot spare the brave sincerity of any
of the humblest or the wisest of mankind. The more honest
and courageous the individual mind, the more excellent will
be the social rationality which is compounded of the thinking of an innumerable company of human beings in the long
years behind us and in this present time. Only let us keep
steadily in mind the fact that ours is pre-eminently a time of
intellectual transition, and be slow to accept any sweeping

generalization, especially if it is subversive of the great faith
and hope to which the social rationality of the human race
has heretofore acceded with something approaching to a
cordial unanimity. There is a day after to-day. The end is
not yet. There is more truth, as Robinson, of Leiden, said,
to break forth from God's word,— not from the Bible only,
but from that book whose leaves are time and space, whose
sentences are writ in constellations and in galaxies upon the
evening skies. If it must needs be that offences come, why
not in our time as well as any? Let us be as patient as we
can under the burden of the mystery. But, while appreci-
ating that every fact indubitably attested is a revelation as
authoritative as if God had rent the heavens and come
down, let us suspend our judgment for a time whenever we
have urged upon us a teaching, be it in the name of science
or theology, that appears to offer us only a mean and paltry
rendering of the universe or of the human soul.

> "The man that went the cloud within
>   Is gone and vanished quite;
> ' He cometh not, the people cries,
>   Nor bringeth God to sight':
> ' Lo! these thy gods, that safety give,
>   Adore and keep the feast,'
> Deluding and deluded, cries
>   The Prophet's brother-priest;
> And Israel all bows down to fall
>   Before the gilded beast.
>
> " Devout, indeed! That priestly creed,
>   O Man, reject as sin;
> The clouded hill attend thou still,
>   And him that went within.
> He yet shall bring some worthy thing
>   For waiting souls to see:
> Some sacred word that he hath heard
>   Their light and life shall be.
> Some lofty part than which the heart
>   Adopt no nobler can,
> Thou shalt receive, thou shalt believe,
>   And thou shalt do, O Man!"

NO BACKWARD STEP.

For some months I have been hearing much of Dr. Gordon's new book, "The Christ of To-day," and have anticipated great pleasure in the reading of it when the convenient season should arrive. Reading it very carefully, I finished it some days ago ; and I propose to make it the subject of my discourse this morning. But why should I do this? Because the book is one of the most significant that have recently appeared ; because it is particularly significant to the Unitarian body, for which it has the finest lot of compliments this body ever has received from such a source, while at the same time it is invited to gird itself like one in solemn haste for its return to the rock from which it was hewn and the pit from which it was digged,—the orthodox conception of Jesus, who is called the Christ. Its author, Dr. George A. Gordon, is the minister of the Old South Church in Boston, the most representative Congregational church in that city, and, consequently, in the United States. He is a man of great ability and culture, a writer of great force and brilliancy, the master of a noble rhetoric and a happy gift of illustration, a preacher whose habitual note is one of profound moral earnestness and spiritual invitation. Moreover, his book is not an isolated product. It is one of many which in these last days are coming in upon us like a flood,—the characteristic books of what is sometimes called Progressive Orthodoxy and sometimes the New Theology. (The second of these names is certainly the better, because "Orthodoxy" and "Progressive" are mutually destructive terms. Orthodoxy ceases to be Orthodoxy the moment it begins to be progressive. Progress ceases to be progress the moment it becomes orthodoxy; *i.e.*, a doctrine which is a dogma because it is held as a finality.)

I am a diligent reader of these books, though, in general, they contribute little to the sweetness of my temper or the improvement of my mind. But they are very interesting to any one who is interested in the stupendous theological transition of the time. It is no exaggeration to say that three or four new ones have come to me in a single day. They are of all degrees of merit, and I will only name some of the most conspicuous of the most recently arrived: "Social Theology," by President Hyde, of Bowdoin College; Dr. Coyle's "Spirit in Literature and Life,"—certain "Rand Lectures," delivered in Iowa College; Rev. Frederic Palmer's "Studies in Theologic Definition"; "The Morals of Evolution," by Professor Harris, of the Andover Theological Seminary; and with these the book to which I am inviting your particular attention. They all agree in being wide departures from the traditional standards of Orthodoxy, but they agree in little else. The departure is in different degrees. The devices whereby the new things are made to look like the old things are extremely various. Here and there a writer is quite indifferent to the old forms of thought, and spends his strength in developing the new ideas. Such an one is Professor Harris, of Andover; and how he can ever sign again the creed which Andover professors are obliged to sign every few years it is impossible to conceive. But the Rev. Frederic Palmer, who is an Episcopalian clergyman in the same town, proposes to go on using the old creeds and articles, with the understanding that they shall be accepted as meaning not what they say, but what they do not say, what the authors of them wanted to say, but couldn't manage to articulate, what they would say if they were living now in Mr. Palmer's skin and with his individual mind.

But Dr. Gordon's book is, if not unique in the advancing host, exceptional in the degree of its insistence on the divinity and deity of Jesus Christ. In Professor Harris's book, as in Dr. Lyman Abbott's " Evolution of Christianity," the specialization of Jesus is simply an arbitrary assertion of his unique perfection,— a perfection, nevertheless, entirely human and attainable by other men, albeit with supreme omniscience we are assured (at least by Dr. Abbott) that no other human being has so far attained an equal height. If deity is predicated of Jesus by writers of this class, it is only in the sense that it is predicable of every human being ; and the predication is built out of the ruins of the traditional doctrine of the depravity of human nature, and on the deep foundation of Channing's "one sublime idea,"— the dignity and grandeur of the human soul. In the Christology of such writers we have a reproduction of the Unitarian thinking midway of the century, when it was freeing itself from the Arian and Socinian traditional forms and endeavoring to find a speculative basis for its emotional persuasion of the singularity of Jesus. It so happens that the Christology of Professor Harris and Dr. Abbott and such men is far more rational and progressive than the Christology of Channing and his contemporaries who agreed with him, and even than the Christology of Dr. Priestley and those who agreed with him. The former was the Arian conception of Jesus as a being *sui generis :* the latter was the Socinian conception of Jesus as a human being exalted to the right hand of God in token of his moral victories over sin and death. But, because the Christology of Progressive Orthodoxy is far more liberal and progressive than that of our early Unitarians, it does not follow that it is any final resting-place for Orthodoxy, any more than it was for Unitarianism when it arrived at it some half a century ago. For this it was a theological Samaria. But it must needs go to Jerusalem. Leaving behind the half-way house that gave it comfort for a while, it must push on to a more rational and consistent doctrine of the humanity of Jesus, a less arbitrary specialization. And we have every reason to believe that it will be as impossible for the New Orthodoxy to go thus far and no farther as it was for the Unitarianism of fifty years back.

But, as I have said, Dr. Gordon's book is not to be confounded with such restatements as Dr. Abbott's and Professor Harris's. It is like them in its general departure from the traditional theology of the Congregational churches. It is unlike them in its persistent and emphatic specialization of Jesus to a degree that makes him absolutely unique in history and in the universe of souls. As compared with the majority of the restatements of Christian doctrine that are in these days "marching single in an endless file," it is, to my apprehension, a restatement of commanding height. It has a positive and affirmative and aggressive air and carriage that are very interesting and engaging, especially in comparison with the compromising, minimizing tactics of some others. And then, too, there is little or nothing of the endeavor, so common and so unlovely and repellent, to put the new wine into old bottles, and label them with the old labels, and powder them with artificial dust, with a nice bit of cobweb here and there,— tricks that are as familiar to the observer of our theological transition as the successions of the day and night. To the extent that Dr. Gordon differs from the traditional theology, his difference is frank and unmistakable ; and there is not the least attempt to make it seem less than it is or to call new things by old misleading names. So far as he affirms the special and unique, divine and deified * character and function of Jesus, he is equally frank and unmistakable ; and, while his goal is that of Orthodoxy all the ages down, he does not pretend for a moment that his path to it coincides precisely with the beaten track. It certainly does not. His despair of that is written upon every page,— not in the way of criticism, but of avoidance and complete neglect. The mighty theologians of the past have "added to him nothing," as Paul said of the apostles at Jerusalem. "Behold," he says, "I show unto you a more excellent way." His book is a tremendous *tour de force*, whereby he is resolved to save, if possible, the threatened

* Not the right word, but there is no better to express something more than divine, the actual deity of Jesus which Dr. Gordon predicates.

citadel of the peculiar and unique pre-eminence of Jesus, even his eternal power and godhead.

I could not, I think, have come to Dr. Gordon's book with a more active prepossession in its favor than actually possessed my mind. I had seen the man, and heard him speak; and there was something in his speech and bearing so strong and masterful, so simple and transparent, that I could expect from him only fine and admirable things. Then, too, I read the book in the warm light of a dear friend's enthusiastic admiration; and that continually gave me pause, and, where my judgment was unfavorable, obliged me to reconsider it, if haply a more favorable judgment might ensue. My favorable prepossession was increased by a wide tumult of acclaim from out the liberal ranks and by the distrust and disapproval of those of high repute for an orthodoxy as immaculate as the new-fallen snow. Last, but not least, my friend Minot J. Savage had said of it in a printed sermon, "There is almost nothing in it which I should wish to attack. . . . I have little else for it than unqualified praise."

Did I expect too much? It is always dangerous to approach a book along an avenue that rings with cries of admiration. I read "Rab and his Friends," for the first time, on the strength of a comment on it, to the effect that any one was less than human who could read it without shedding tears. Less than human I was obliged to think myself, for not one bedewed my cheek. (Another time I had a different experience.) Whatever the reason, I am obliged to say that Dr. Gordon's book has grievously disappointed me. I did not expect it to reverse all the deep-seated habits of my theological belief. But I did expect a more serious and imposing challenge of these habits than I found in the event. Its rhetorical mountains are lofty, but the arguments are mean. The texture of the book is that of a web heavy with gold and precious stones, but so rotten in its fibre that it falls to pieces in the admirer's careful hands. Unconsciously, the writer has endeavored to make up for the pov-

erty of his reasoning by the splendor of his imagery and
style; and many will, no doubt, be more than pleased and
satisfied to accept in lieu of bread the jewels that are scattered with a lavish hand. Others will be more exigent.
Cardinal Newman has a noble sermon upon "Unreal
Words." Seldom have I read a book in which I have
seemed to find so many as in Dr. Gordon's "Christ of
To-day." It is as full of unreal thinking as an egg is full of
meat. It is smitten through and through with unreality.
Often, where there is most show of argument, we have a mere
juggle of words. Often, where the argument becomes most
tenuous, it is wound about with iridescent films of lovely
and beguiling speech, or suddenly we are invested in a rosy
mist, or dazzled with a blaze of rhetoric that makes men
appear as trees walking and everything uncertain and obscure. Not for a moment do I imagine that there is any
conscious and deliberate device in this. "It is an insult to
allow that we are honest," Channing said; and, if Dr. Gordon should resent my disavowal in this manly fashion, I
should not think it strange. But, as the eye spontaneously
closes to defend itself against any danger from without, so
I am obliged to feel that Dr. Gordon's mind, in the passionate ardor of his desire to rehabilitate a tottering theology,
has closed spontaneously at the approach of anything that
made against his preconceived opinion, and opened only to
what seemed to favor it; and not only so, but that he has
a rhetorical astigmatization which magnifies a hundred-fold
whatever favors his foregone conclusion, and correspond-
ingly diminishes whatever fact is prejudicial thereunto.

But as yet I have not sounded the depths of my disappointment in Dr. Gordon's brilliant and (for all its limitations) fascinating performance. I go a little deeper when I
remark that I find in its central argument nothing of that
scientific method which the opening pages led me to expect
in the discussion of the lofty theme. I am reminded of that
"Christian Science," which, however Christian it may be, has
nothing in its method which an instructed man of science

would recognize as having the least affinity with the patient methods of his class and school. Everywhere we have "a ladder let down" from an imaginary height, and dangling in the air; everywhere the "high *priori* road," the strenuous endeavor to compel the echo of a foregone conclusion from the facts,—and not a patient scientific investigation of the facts, if haply, knowing what they are, we may adjust ourselves to them with a courageous heart. In what some would fain imagine they have found the radiant morning of a new day of scientific Christianity I can only find the splendid sunset of the long cloudy day of mediæval theology, pre-scientific thought; the last attenuation, elusive, vague, impalpable, of a belief which once was solid to men's grasp and like the earth under their weary feet.

Let me, in passing, beg you to notice this,—and you cannot notice it too carefully: that, whatever the intrinsic merit of Dr. Gordon's conception of Jesus, it is a pure speculation. It has so much value, and no more, as his private thought can give it, his personal argument. It has no dogmatic value whatsoever. All of the old supports are gone. The Bible has for him no supernatural character or authority. For the old "Thus saith the Lord" we have simply, "Thus saith Dr. Gordon." And, if his results are generally accepted, they must be accepted solely upon his authority by nine hundred and ninety-nine out of a thousand people. Even if his argument is valid, there are not two persons in a thousand who can appreciate its force, so vague is it, so mystical. It is hard to answer such a book. As the Spanish proverb says, "You cannot take soft cheese upon a hook." Propositions to be answerable must, first of all, be apprehensible. And Dr. Gordon's frequently are not. They may be to him: they certainly are not to me. The fault may be entirely on my side. Like foolish Ixion, I embrace a cloud. But my self-respect demands that I should not consider myself entirely singular in this regard. Wherefore, I hope and trust that we have not here the last word of Orthodoxy, if Orthodoxy is to dominate the world for any length of coming time. If we are to have no more of dogma, no more finality, no more of irrational or ultra-rational or supernatural authority, then, unless the hungry sheep are to look up and be not fed, if the common people are to hear the gospel gladly, and with an understanding mind, the statement that is to attract and hold them and bind them in a high allegiance and a holy trust has got to be something ten times, a hundred times, a thousand times, more clear and simple and straightforward than Dr. Gordon's magnificent obscurity and incomprehensible sublimity.

I go deeper still in fathoming my disappointment when I say, as say I must in all sincerity, that Dr. Gordon has not succeeded in developing a conception of Jesus,—"of the Christ," I ought to say, for there is little or nothing of Jesus in the vast ethereal abstraction which he has substituted for his sweet human worth,—he has not succeeded in developing a conception of the Christ which can be relied upon to touch the common heart, or indeed more than a few people of exceptional imaginative genius or power of theosophic speculation. Many will complain, as one did in the New Testament legend, "They have taken away my Lord, and I know not where they have laid him." Dr. Gordon has taken Jesus away from the familiar earth and all the sweet habitudes of its experience, and wrapped him in a winding-sheet of cloudy speculation, and buried him in some hollow cave between the confines of the human and divine, forever inaccessible to men and women to whom he cannot lend his mighty pinions and his winged heels. I know well enough the limitations of Renan's portraiture of Jesus ; but, passing almost directly from that — as brightened and renewed by Dr. Allen's careful hand — to Dr. Gordon's rhapsodic variation on the immortal theme, I must confess that it is vastly more attractive to my imagination and appealing to my heart. Over and over again, a thousand times, we have had it pleaded that the Nicene theology saved the humanity of Jesus even while insisting on his deity. It was for this reason that Dr. Hedge and other Unitarians were more attracted to it than to the Arian conception, which interprets Jesus as a being *sui generis*, — as one * said, "but an iota less than God." But Dr. Gordon's Christ is as "remote from the sphere of our sorrow" as the Christ of Arius. If here and there his humanity is verbally expressed, the expression is a mere logomachy. The whole stress of the argument is on his singularity, his divinity, his deity, with immense rhetorical agility the writer swinging himself back and forth between these various expressions.

Let me quote a sentence here and there which bears upon this matter : "The ultimateness of Christ's thought and the finality of his spirit differentiate his transcendence from the greatest and best of mankind, and ground his being in the Godhead in a way solitary and supreme." I will not pause to show how unscientific and unsatisfactory are the arguments, if arguments they can be called, for such ultimateness and such finality, but pass on to other sentences which endeavor to assimilate this idea of a supreme and solitary Jesus, unique, divine, yea, "very God of very God," in a manner wholly peculiar to himself, to the idea of Jesus as a human being. For example, "That our Lord is the moral ideal of humanity implies these two things, — that he is one with humanity and that he transcends it infinitely." If we have not here a contradiction in terms, I do not know the meaning of the words. Again, in the same manner, "He is the perfect humanity after which we must forever strive. and short of which we must forever fall."

> "Chip, chop, chain ;
> Give a thing and take it back again."

Such is the method over and over again in this discussion. Dr. Gordon is an Hegelian of the Hegelians in his confidence that the unity of truth is made up of contradictory propositions. Thus, "The mere fact of Christ's transcendence of earthly conditions joins him to the race of which he is a perfect specimen : the extent and character of this trans-

* Dr. Francis Parkman.

cendence call for a deeper origin in God for him than for the rest of mankind." If there is any meaning in these words, it is entirely past my finding out.* So, again, where we are told : "Only a Christ whose antithesis to humanity means the presence of the very God can by his union with humanity assure us of union with God. Discredit the infinite difference, and we must doubt the sublime identity." Words, words, words ! If Dr. Gordon has succeeded in deifying Jesus, he has succeeded at the same time in utterly dehumanizing him and in robbing humanity of any help that Jesus has seemed to offer heretofore to the confirmation of its natural heredity from God.

The fine things which Dr. Gordon has said about Unitarianism and Unitarians have, I fear, so dazzled many of our people that they have had no eyes to see his fundamental propositions, and the stupendous differentiation of his thought and purpose from that of the Unitarian movement in the present stage of its advance. That his words concerning us are very fine there is no doubt. Fairer have never yet been spoken by a preacher of commanding orthodox position, and that the preacher of the Old South should have given them utterance is something marvellous. One passage is as follows : —

Any words of mine bearing upon Unitarianism are written, I trust it is needless to say, in honor and gratitude for the great movement of thought whose power for good has been so vast, but from whose conception of Christ I differ. Mutual recognition is the basis of all fruitful discussion. As a tenacious Trinitarian, I rejoice to recognize the benefit to the Christian Church of the Unitarian contention. No intelligent religious person can fail to honor its insistence upon the Fatherhood of God, the real and therefore the divine humanity of our Lord, the function of history as a revelation of God, the place of the Bible at the centre of religious history, and salvation as a moral process under the Spirit of God. Against a Trinitarianism that was tritheism, in opposition to a view of the person of Christ that slighted his humanity and dishonored the Eternal Father, in the face of opinions that made history godless and terrible ; that construed salvation as outward, forensic, mechanical ; that

* But they are the key-stone of his argument, and that is strong only as they are strong.

regarded religion as alien to the nature of man, at war with the intellectual and moral wealth of the world, and that turned it into a provincial and deformed thing,— the Unitarian protest was wholesome, magnificent, providential.

Even less remarkable is the cordial recognition in this passage of the good things which Unitarians have done than the indictment that is brought against traditional Orthodoxy. Surely, no Unitarian has ever brought against it a more terrible indictment, not Theodore Parker in his utmost joy of battle. Another passage varies the form of this indictment, but maintains its spirit, and reiterates the praise of Unitarian truth. Here it is : —

Under the supremacy of the Augustinian and Calvinistic conception of human nature, the consciousness of sin necessarily tends to become exclusive, and the task of Christian living to become more and more a lamentation over the defect of character and a despair of goodness. More and more salvation must become, not the act by which God educates his children and claims his own, but the triumph of Almighty pity over sheer worthlessness. This overdone sense of depravity, hardened into dogma, stood for centuries against the truth that the morality of God in Christ is the morality for mankind. The truth has at last prevailed, and at this point of belief Christian people everywhere are under an immense debt to the great Unitarian leaders.

Listen to this also, which does not more generously praise our Unitarian leaders than it condemns the orthodox position upon which they trained their guns : —

Channing and Hedge and Peabody and Furness, and their contemporaries, refused to be forever shut up within the consciousness of moral defect and infirmity. They held that the morality of Jesus has power to give life to the spirit to which it comes ; that it elicits into clearness and strength the aboriginal human endowment, sets free the divine in man's constitution, and invests it with new vigor and prophetic invincibility. The leaders of the Unitarian movement were men of exalted spirit ; in them the ethical and religious principles lived in great power. They were unimpeachable examples of the high doctrine that they proclaimed.

We cannot be too grateful for this liberal appreciation, and we cannot but be glad when a distinguished orthodox preacher adopts the Unitarian criticism of the five points of

Calvinism, the Universalist doctrine of the salvation of mankind, the opinions which the higher criticism has developed concerning the Bible in general and its various parts; and some of you, perhaps, will think that it is most ungracious and ungrateful in me, where such immense concessions have been made and such fine compliments have been bestowed, to take a critical attitude, and put my emphasis on those things which differentiate the thought of Dr. Gordon's book from that of the consistent modern Unitarian. But, in doing this, I only do what Dr. Gordon has done himself. He has not spent his strength in complimenting Unitarians on the virtues of their leaders and their sires, nor in laying bare the hideous deformity of the theology of Augustine, Calvin, and Edwards. The expression on these lines is brief and incidental. When he girds up his loins like a man, and says, " I will speak, and answer thou me," it is to frankly state his difference from our Unitarian position in respect to the humanity of Jesus. To repeat what I have said already. In its main purpose and its almost exclusive emphasis his book is a tremendous *tour de force*, whereby he is resolved to save, if possible, the threatened citadel of the peculiar and unique pre-eminence of Jesus, and ally him and identify him with the Deity in a manner wholly unparalleled by any human being, and impossible for any such. And not only so, but Dr. Gordon's book is the frankest possible challenge to the modern Unitarian to accept his doctrine of the peculiar divinity and deity of Jesus, or perish for his fault. He says, " The Unitarian movement has its opportunity here : it must contemplate some kind of a return,— a return consistent with its magnificent protest and achievement,— or it must engage in a serious meditation with death." Not to accept so frank a challenge would be simply pusillanimous.

I must confess that my impression of the book is very different from Mr. Savage's, who says, as we have seen, that he finds " little in it to attack," that he has " little else for it than unqualified praise." Comparing it with Theodore Parker's epoch-making sermon of 1841, " The Transient and

Permanent in Christianity," he says that that "was not nearly so radical as related to the theology of that time as Dr. Gordon's book is as related to the theology of our time." I wonder how he could say that. I should say that not only was Parker's sermon more radical in its day than Gordon's book in ours, but that Parker's sermon preached in our day would be much more radical than Gordon's book. For, though Dr. Gordon's book is radical enough in its conceptions of the Bible and revelation and total depravity and sacrificial atonement, it is immensely, strikingly, magnificently unradical, conservative, reactionary, traditional, orthodox, in its conception of Jesus of Nazareth and his relations to humanity and God.

The arguments by which Dr. Gordon endeavors to establish the unique divinity and deity of Jesus are anything but stale. They are wonderfully fresh and new. They take up into themselves what is favorable to them in modern thought, as the purple ash takes from the soil the color of its leaf, the rose the blood-red of its heart. There is nothing of the old marshalling of texts. If texts are quoted here and there, it is in a poet's fashion, as no one has ever quoted them before or will again. It is not a little strange that a doctrine which has been prominent in Christendom for fifteen hundred years should find all its historical foundations rotten, and require others, quarried from the most superficial deposits of the modern mind. But one advantage of this situation is that, gravitating to all that is most noble and encouraging in modern thought, Dr. Gordon's book abounds in happy inspirations. The way he travels may not reach the goal of his desire ; but in the mean time it is generally a very pleasant way, opening out here and there on landscapes of great breadth and beauty, with flowers at every turn that have the color of the writer's mind, the fragrance of his heart.

It is not an easy thing to reproduce the argument of Dr. Gordon. To reproduce the music of an organ out of church would be hardly more difficult, so set to music is his thought,— the music of a beautiful and noble style. He begins with the assertion that "certain great advances have been made in the appreciation of the person" of Jesus. First, as Channing phrased it, "the imitableness of Christ's character." "This, once an exclusive Unitarian possession, is now," says Dr. Gordon, "the common property of all Christians." "The second great gain," he says, "lies in the representative character of Christ, Godward." He is not the only son of God. The universal sonship of mankind is written in his face. So far we have good Unitarian thinking, and it is interesting to our curiosity to see how by such steps Dr. Gordon can get any nearer to the deity of Jesus and his "social" position in the blessed Trinity. Another great gain, he says, is that "it is now becoming clear that the final meaning of nature and the character of ultimate reality are given through Christ." Nothing could exceed the looseness in the development of this proposition. It is simply monstrous to say that, "by all believers in God in our western world, Christ's intelligence and will have been selected as representing the Supreme Intelligence and will"; and the looseness becomes absurd, if not immoral, when Shelley and Emerson are cited with Wordsworth and Tennyson and Browning as "beholding in nature one vast form of the Eternal Christ." In this connection the scientific arraignment of nature comes up to be judged. Dr. Gordon calls it a "horrible caricature," and tells us that a different view is "beginning to control our thoughts," the view of Professor Drummond, in his "Ascent of Man," that there is in nature "a struggle for others," as well as the mere egotistic, selfish struggle for existence. But what is a mere beginning on page 88, on page 92 is a perfect consummation. "Our universe," he says, "is now Christomorphic"; *i.e*, it has the form of Christ's intelligence and love. This upon the strength of a few brave endeavors to withstand the swelling tide of pessimistic science. I have the liveliest sympathy with those endeavors. But I am appalled at Dr. Gordon's putting the goodness and beneficence and tenderness of nature to a vote, and declaring a unanimous affirmative, when Huxley was but one of many who have had the conclusion that the universe is unloving, cruel, anti-ethical, forced upon their minds; and to affirm that the natural order has "the mind of Christ," even if the tide of pessimistic science had been turned back victoriously, is to use the name of Christ so loosely that it becomes a delusion and a snare which every one believing in clear thinking should avoid.

A chain is no stronger than its weakest link, and that, in Dr. Gordon's "three great advances," is his last. The first and second are advances in the Unitarian direction. The imitableness of Christ's character and his representative sonship are Unitarian ideas of such early date that the patent on them has run out. The third of Dr. Gordon's "three great advances" involves so much looseness, vagueness, and assumption that I cannot conceive that it would have value for any one who has a predilection for clear and definite thought. I cannot conceive how Dr. Gordon himself can put it forth as a piece of valid thinking. But, even if it were entirely valid, and the universe were proved to have a loving heart, there would not be the least advance, "not in the estimation of a hair," toward the enormous specialization of Jesus which is the "butt and sea-mark of his utmost sail."

Dr. Gordon is himself of this opinion. Beyond the three advances specified he tells us "all is dark"; and they do not, he says, bring us to any essential difference in Jesus from mankind, "any relationship to the Deity that sets him apart from mankind, any attribute in virtue of which he is the Eternal Son of God." To establish this essential difference, this peculiar relationship, this special attribute, is the main purpose of Dr. Gordon's book. How does he go to work?

In the first place, he says that to deny the possible supreme divinity of Jesus means the destruction of all individuality. That may convey no meaning to your minds. The meaning is that, if men are not all alike, if there are innumerable degrees of personality, one may be supremely good; and that one may have been Jesus. I think that we shall none of us object to that. But so far we have only possibility, and a possibility which, if converted into certainty, would not involve the essential difference from mankind, the peculiar relationship to God, the special attribute of eternal sonship, which Dr. Gordon attributes to Jesus, and would fain confirm as his inviolable trust. And, if it did, the deity of Jesus, of which Dr. Gordon freely allows himself to speak, would be almost as remote as ever. But how does he convert his possibility of the unique supremacy of Jesus in the universe of souls into the certainty of this? He shall answer for himself in his own words: "The path to this eternal contrast between Christ and all the other sons of God is his perfect humanity." We have a pure assumption here — that perfect humanity dehumanizes. I should consider it much more rational to affirm that the most imperfect humanity does so. But here is a test which, working it either way, would reduce the limits of humanity to those of the Scotch orthodox kirk, "me and Sandy," with a doubt whether Sandy was quite orthodox. When Dr. Soule at Exeter proposed to expel one of the boys because he was the lowest in the class, the boy fell back upon his ounce of mother wit, and said, "If you keep that up, you won't have anybody left." Eliminate Jesus from humanity as the highest of mankind, and you have as good reason for eliminating the next highest, and so on.*

Dr. Gordon's supreme divinity of Jesus rests upon his perfect humanity. Here is the elephant, and here are the four tortoises; and what next? What do the four tortoises rest upon? How prove the perfect humanity of Jesus? "The scheme that is to prevail, that is not doomed to a disastrous collision with reality, must grow [it is Dr. Gordon who says so] out of the historic truth." Now, the historic truth concerning Jesus is found in the New Testament. All that is there is not historic truth, but there is no historic truth about Jesus that is not there. Do we find the perfect

---

* This is a homely illustration, but is not homelier, I think, than Dr. Gordon's "grin without a cat,"—"the classic illustration of Alice in Wonderland,"— to express the futility of an exalted moral ideal without the personal Jesus.

humanity of Jesus in the New Testament, when we have stripped away what is most obviously the accretion of a credulous imagination? Can we conceive of perfect manhood without that quality of fatherhood from which Jesus drew his image of the Divine Perfection,— without the realization of those glorious passions which are the master passions of the human heart? Moreover, are there not things written of Jesus which, if they are true, take something from the fulness of his perfection? And one thing is sure,— that Jesus did not consider himself perfect. He said: "Why callest thou me good? There is none good but one, and that is God." Those are as certainly the words of Jesus as any in the New Testament, because they would certainly never have been *invented* by his admiring followers. They stand so in *Mark*. In *Matthew* we can see the endeavor to break their force: "Why speakest thou to me of the good?" It would be strange if the idealizing temper of the apostolic age left anything in the record that could suggest a doubt to that age of the moral perfection of Jesus. Probably it did not, with the exception of the disavowal to which I have referred. But however little the defect, and however beautiful and glorious and tender the positive excellence disclosed, appealing, as Dr. Gordon says we must, to historic truth, I must confess — and here I know that I am one of many — that I do not find anything in the New Testament to establish, *or even to suggest*, the essential moral difference of Jesus from the best and greatest of mankind. But that is because moral excellence is never a surprise to me. I expect it, just as I expect the sun to rise, the stars to shine, the springtime or the falling snow to be most fair. I have seen too much of it in history and in my own personal experience to be astounded by its most lovely manifestations. What I *am* astounded at is that any one imbued with the critical and scientific spirit should find it necessary to isolate Jesus, separating him from the great human order. Seen in the light of critical research, he stands as naturally in the human order as the trees stand in the woods. There are human personalities which are much more baffling than his in their source and stream.

The fact is we have discovered what Dr. Gordon's four tortoises — the perfect humanity of Jesus — are resting on. It is not on the historic truth of the New Testament. It is on his theological inheritance of the Calvinistic persuasion of human incompetency and depravity. Nowhere is he more eloquent than where he is discarding this persuasion. But it is one thing to intellectually disown a traditional doctrine, and another thing to free one's self from its unconscious working in our thought. The bed-rock of Dr. Gordon's book is his inability to think greatly of mankind, to expect from it a sublime morality. He frees himself in words from the besetting sin only to find his thought enmeshed with it a moment hence. He praises Channing for his lofty affirmation of the dignity of human nature, but he never is possessed by his spirit. If he had been, his work would never have been written. The moral excellence of Jesus never would have suggested his essential difference from the best and wisest of mankind.

To sum up, Dr. Gordon has "three great advances" in the appreciation of Jesus, two of which are commonplaces of Unitarian belief,—"the imitableness of Christ's character" and the universal sonship of mankind; while the third,— the heart of nature, the heart of Christ,— is too vaguely stated and too loosely reasoned to deserve consideration. Wherefore at this point everything remains for him to do along his special line. First, from the richness of the diversity of human character he infers that one human being may exceed all others, and that Jesus may be this one. Then by the high *priori* road, with supreme indifference to the New Testament history, he arrives at the perfect humanity of Jesus,— a perfection which isolates him from all others, makes him absolutely unique, and not only the peculiar Son of God, but God himself. For the later stages of this journey we have beautiful words, with no corresponding realities of intellectual seriousness. Between the perfect humanity of Jesus and his deity there is a great gulf fixed, which Dr. Gordon spans by a gossamer bridge, to which we are invited to intrust ourselves. But we decline with thanks.

But the whole argument is of the flimsiest. In the first place, upon the rich diversity of human nature is based the possible supremacy of Jesus. In the second place, this supremacy is made the basis of his separateness from humanity and his unique relation to God. Could any two premises be more absolutely exclusive and destructive of each other? Finally, for the unique perfection of Jesus we have no appeal to history, but an argument whose silent major premise is the Augustinian, Calvinistic, Edwardsean distrust of human nature, which Dr. Gordon formally rejects, but unconsciously reproduces upon every page.

No backward step! If the alternative to such a method and conception as Dr. Gordon offers us is, as he says, "a serious meditation with death," then be it this. It will then be at least "serious"; and *that* his method is not, and his conception is not. But I, for one, do not believe that "a serious meditation with death" is the only alternative to our acceptance of an unserious scheme of thought, or to any sort of a return to the traditional theology. The Unitarian opportunity is *not* here, but in a conception of humanity so generous and so expectant that the lofty and inspiring excellence of Jesus shall be to us more natural and human than the baseness of the wicked and the vileness of the vile, and in a conception of the Incarnation that must have ampler evidence of the Human Heart of God than is supplied by one supreme attainment,—even so much as glows and shines and burns for us in the unnumbered lives of those who have lifted up their hearts to great ideals, and have embodied them in the joy and sorrow, in the struggle and the anguish, in the yearning and devotion, of their daily walk with God.

GRAVITATIONS OF THE SPIRIT.

WHEN we read in the New Testament, "To him that hath shall be given, and from him that hath not shall be taken away even that which he hath," we may think that we have here a hard saying; but we are constrained to recognize that it has in it a great deal of truth. It is the conclusion of a parable based upon the aggregating quality of money; and no one, I imagine, will deny that the parable was well conceived. The destruction of the poor is their poverty. Everything costs them more because they have to purchase it in the smallest quantities. The shabby clothes stand in the way of the employment which would make better possible. The lack of capital handicaps the smaller manufacturers and tradesmen in the race. The big fish eat up the little ones: we have many kinds of business in one, and the great trusts annihilating individuals to left and right. The more gigantic these, the greater their capacity for absorbing enterprises of more modest character into their portentous bulk. So with the private fortune.* Once a certain point is reached, and under normal conditions the great financier has little more to do than sit beside his nectar, and see his wealth making itself greater by spontaneous aggregation. While he is musing, the fire burns. And what is true in these particulars is true of every kind of individual and social aggregation. Let the preacher attract a thousand hearers, and another thousand will come easily enough. Let the magazine or newspaper get one hundred thousand subscribers, and another hundred thousand comes inevitably.

* I have read in the Life of Samuel Tilden that what he left increased from five to seven millions in the short time between his death and the final judgment of the courts which robbed his benevolent intentions of one-half their moral force.

"Trilby" or some other novel of the day runs up a sale of fifty thousand copies. Whereupon another fifty thousand is secure, and another hundred on the hundred thus attained. The Bible asks, "Is not a man much better than a sheep?" In one particular they are very much alike. If anything, man is the more imitative of the two.

It is very interesting to see how soon men's dominant tastes and admirations become principles of aggregation in their lives. No one liked a pleasant story better than Dr. Furness, and consequently his many were continually gathering more. When his friends heard of a new one, they were unhappy until they had imparted it to him. When I went to see him on his ninety-third birthday, he had two or three which he had just added to his collection,—one of the lofty carriage of a darling little fellow, three or four years old, and very near to death, whose trained nurse, a stranger in the house, had called him a baby. "Show her my trousers," he said to his mother, reporting the indignity. The same principles operated with Dr. Furness in the matter of his New Testament criticism. His friends were always bringing to him reports and incidents that fitted into his theory, like a hand into a glove. And, if ever it received a wound, he had only to stretch out his hand, as Thoreau did when he got a fall in Tuckerman's Ravine, and there was the *Arnica mollis*, the very thing he needed for his hurt.

It is with reputations as it is with personal experience. They grow by the attraction of their quality. How many cynical observations have been attributed to Rochefoucauld that are not his! How many witticisims to Sydney Smith! How many homely parables to Abraham Lincoln! One might say without exaggeration that here is a key that unlocks more mysteries of literary aggregation in the Bible than any other. Moses — rightly enough, perhaps — acquired the reputation of being a law-giver. Hence century after century laws were credited to his genius and received the stamp of his authority with which he had nothing to do. In 620 B.C. the whole book of Deuteronomy was attributed

to him, and that made it the most easy and natural thing in
the world to attribute to him *en bloc* the whole Levitic legislation which we have in Numbers and Leviticus. In the
same way David got the reputation of being a hymn-maker,
a psalmist; and, of our one hundred and fifty Psalms,
seventy-three are attributed to him, while the tendency of
our most learned criticism is to put the entire Psalter on this
side of the exile,— that is to say, five centuries later than
his time; if averaged, six or seven. The case of Solomon
is precisely similar. His was a reputation for proverbial
wisdom; and so a Book of Proverbs, which is made up of
several other books, and which was the growth of centuries,
was attributed to him, and not only that, but Ecclesiastes,
because of its proverbial character, and the Wisdom of Solomon, for the same reason, and the Song of Songs, because
it seemed to be a good deal in his line. There are many
other illustrations of this principle of qualitative aggregation
in the Bible. Two-thirds of the Book of Isaiah have got
there in this way, much of Job, Zechariah, Micah, some of
Jeremiah, and so on.

This kind of thing has both absurd and painful illustrations in our every-day affairs. Reputations are built up by
it, and others are destroyed. A rolling stone gathers no
moss, but a revolving rumor gathers abundant incident and
confirmation. Given the disposition to believe well or ill
of any one, and the pound gathers ten pounds very soon. ·
The testimony to which we should not give the slightest
heed, as against our own political chief, would be utterly
damning for us, as against a political opponent. *Fere liben-
ter homines id quod volunt credunt.* I remember so much of
Cæsar's Gallic Commentaries the more easily because it has
been rubbed into me by the experience of forty years.
" Men very readily believe that which they want to."

In short, to him that hath shall be given. It is a principle
of spiritual gravitation which finds its illustrations in a hundred different aspects of the intellectual and moral life of
individuals. It is the principle of inertia and the law of the

least resistance carried over from the material into the spiritual sphere. Every physical body has a disposition to maintain the condition in which it finds itself. That is the principle of inertia. It is commonly understood to mean only that bodies have a disposition to remain immovable and unchanged. And this misunderstanding is carried over into the metaphorical meanings of the word ; and, when we say that a man is inert, we mean that he is sluggish, dull, immovable. But there is as much inertia in a physical body's disposition to go on in the way it is going as to remain in the position in which it is. As with the physical inertia, so with the spiritual, for which Habit is another name. Every habit — idleness, industry, generosity, meanness, intemperance, temperance, selfishness, benevolence — tends to its own perpetuation and increase. If you don't want to *be* a thing, then do not *do* it many times. If the line of the least resistance manifestly leads to physical or intellectual or moral ruin, then — right about face !

We are permitted not only to perceive that these things are so, but, to some extent, how they are so. Like loveth like, the proverb says, or, should I say, the poet sings? There is a proverb that says something to the same effect : " Birds of a feather flock together."

Now there is warning here, as well as simple and indifferent fact. We must beware of the fatality of an environment selected by our dominant tendencies of thought and feeling. When we discover that we are having everything pretty much our own way, that all is grist that comes to our mill, that almost everything we read and almost every one we meet tends to confirm us in our personal opinion, we must begin to suspect ourselves, to ask whether we are not following too complacently the line of the least resistance, seeking too much the sympathy of those who are likely to agree with us, or for the sake of good fellowship avoiding grounds of difference with our acquaintances and friends. Friendship is hardly worth the having that puts a padlock on our lips. Far better that which is equal to the stress and strain of manly difference !

To him that hath shall be given. The *modus operandi*
in the sphere of public thought and action is as clear as
clear can be. The belief or policy once dominant becomes selective of our environment of men or books; and
this re-enforces our belief, strengthens our confidence in our
policy, whatever it may be. We read the newspapers, the
arguments, the speeches, that will confirm us in our faith;
and we give a wide berth to those of a different and opposing character. So doing, we follow the line of the least
resistance. As with matters of public thought and action,
so with matters of the pure intellect, and with matters of
social theory and religious doctrine and observance. I look
into my own heart, and write. My inclination is to read the
books that will confirm my well-established thought, philosophic, economic, theological. I dare not say that I should
not have been the chief of sinners in this kind but for my
happy fortune as a reviewer of many books. As they come
to me, they are of all kinds,— realistic, idealistic, experiential,
intuitional, socialistic, individualistic, conservative, heretical,
theistic, atheistic, and so on. And the consequence is that
I am not so cock-sure, so absolutely certain, so dogmatic
about many things as I might otherwise be. For there are
a good many things which, to feel entirely sure about, you
must only read one book or one set of books. If you read
more, you will have to stop and think ; and before you know
it you will have "the fatal disqualification of seeing the
other side." But there are great compensations in the
wider view. It is destructive of Carlyle's estimate of the
human population, "mostly fools." You find that people
who have ten times your brains and your patience of investigation have not arrived at your opinions ; and, though it may
still be hard for you to see how this one or that can think
as he does theologically, or, thinking as he does, stay where
he is, it is not so hard as it would be without this discipline.
If there is any one set of books that has helped me more
than others, it is the biographies of men distinguished in the
different religious sects. They have not made me doubt —

no, never for an hour — the essential soundness of my Unitarian faith; but they have enabled me to see to what extent men's theological beliefs are symbolical, and how sweet and excellent the things they symbolize may be, while to the symbol itself one is not attracted in the least. And they enable you to see how wonderfully the character and life transcend their doctrinal concomitants. When, as a little boy, I asked the apothecary to put a "libel" on the bottle, he seemed to be amused; but that theological labels are very often, if not generally, libels I have since found to be a good saying and worthy of all acceptation.

As it is in intellectual matters, so is it in the moral. You know about the Concord woman who said to Emerson, "When you enter a room, I resolve that I will try to make human nature seem beautiful to you." I could wish that she had done so, and succeeded, and not said anything about it. Doubtless there are many who have worked the mystery this wise, perhaps unconsciously. That is the way of the world. If men expect goodness and nobility, it comes to them, like doves to the windows. If they expect things hateful and unclean, such rain upon them. Max Nordau has a fixed idea that degeneracy is the salient feature of the closing century. So possessed is he with this idea that his own sanity is endangered, and is sometimes seriously impeached; but on this account its attractive force is not less conspicuous. He finds all the facts he wants to justify his preconception. The excesses and mistakes of genius make genius itself intolerable to him; and he hails the utter lack of it in Mr. Alfred Austin as a delightful omen of the day when the kingdoms of this world shall become the kingdoms of Commonplace, and Dulness shall enjoy a universal reign. So it was with Schopenhauer. He was just the man to whom to turn one's seamy side; and, consequently, for confirmation of his pessimism he did not lack. You know there was a Scotch woman who said of her minister that, if there was a cross text in the Bible, he would be sure to find it for his sermon. But given a man or woman who believes in human goodness heartily, and life seems to organize itself into a conspiracy about them to sustain their cheerful faith. For them there are no bearers of ill tidings. All their friends are like the sparrow that the Greek orator saw midway of his oration, and stopped to say, " I see in the court-yard a sparrow that has seen a slave spilling a sack of corn, and he has gone to tell his fellows." Sure enough he had, and back he came with them to riot in the bounteous store. Such hearers of good tidings are not few. Goodness attracts goodness, kindness attracts kindness, love attracts love. Attracts! It does more than that. It creates it, teases it from what seems the most reluctant soil. I have read a story * of a man who was a potter, and who had a "wee lad" at home, who was frail and sick and never likely to get well. And every night he carried home to him some pretty little thing,— a bit of colored glass, perhaps a flower,— anything bright and cheerful that could lie on the white counterpane in the narrow room, and help to wear away the long and tedious days. Pretty soon the other workmen in the shop got wind of what was going on, and they were not going to be left out. They made little jars and cups, and stuck them in the corners of the kiln at baking time ; and, when these had been taken out and cooled, they put them in the poor man's hat or somewhere where he would know that they were meant for him to take and carry home. They did the same with pictures and with flowers. Not a day went by without some token of their silent sympathy. For it was silent, for the most part, on both sides. The wee lad's father was a man of few words ; and, even when the others took a little of their leisure to do something that would shorten his day's work, so that he might have more time at home, he hadn't much to say. And he had still less, and yet enough, one day, to tell them that

---

* In the volume of Rev. Oscar C. McCulloch's beautiful discourses, where it is given as " cut from a paper " ; but the form, I think, which I have not followed closely, is Mr. McCulloch's. His book, "The Open Door," should have a hundred readers where it has but one.

the little boy was dead ; and when, a day or two later, the bell tolled for the funeral, just around the corner from the shabby door there were a hundred of the workmen, all in their best clothes, waiting till the tiny coffin was brought out, and then falling into line and walking to the grave. It cost them a half day's work to do this gentle office ; but when did ever poor men stand upon a thing like that? And so again it was fulfilled as it is written, "A little child shall lead them."

And now do you know that in such a story as this which I have told it seems to me we have in little all the sphere of human life. The whole round world is but a pottery in which some workman always has a "wee lad" sick, or a poor wife ailing and broken, or some other trouble ; and, given a faithful, loving heart, the gravitation of the planets is not surer than that sympathy and love and help will gravitate to it, and, so doing, build up the man or woman to whom such things come into a sweeter faith, a nobler purpose, and a better life. Human nature and human life, in general, is for the most of us only our personal experience of human nature and of human life writ large ; and men's faith in God is generally much or little in proportion to their faith in human kind. Supposing any one could have made the poor man of my story understand the pessimism of Schopenhauer and Hartmann, do you imagine that he could have been made to believe it? I do not. Nor the atheism of some others. This is the true revelation of the Father in the Son of which we hear so much,— the revelation of the divine in the human. Only thank God, and thank a multitude of men and women that no man can number, that the revelation is not confined to one Son of God who lived and loved and taught and died in far-away Judea eighteen centuries ago, and that he was not even the first-born of many brethren, seeing that thousands before him had shown little or much of the Eternal Goodness, and men and women had rejoiced to see *their* day. And when, as now often happens, well-meaning persons tell us, "Yes, we know all that; but we prefer to use the ancient doctrine as a symbol of the modern thought," happy are we if grace is given to us to say, "I pray thee have me excused," or "Get thee behind me, Satan," or words to that effect. For the doctrine that Jesus is "the only begotten of the Father" is no more a fitting symbol of the universal sonship of humanity than a brick is a fitting symbol of a house or a unit of a million; and the revelation of God in Jesus is no more a fitting symbol of the revelation of God in humanity than one perfect rose is a fitting symbol of the boundless wealth of June and all the summers that have ever come and gone.

You will think, perhaps, that I have left my story of the kindly potters far behind; but I will return to it for a moment, just to say a word that may not be altogether pertinent, but which I am moved to say, which I am always moved to say, as I have opportunity. It is that those workmen in the pottery were, probably, miserably imperfect men. I have not the least doubt that they drank and swore and did other equally disreputable things. But on this account my faith is in no wise shaken in the goodness of their particular conduct in the case of their companion and his suffering child. As it was there, so it is everywhere. I find few perfect men and women. Some of the most respectable would not bear turning inside out so well as some of the most disreputable. But few, if any, are without some better part, which only waits for the appropriate touch to openly declare itself.

That the laws of health and the laws of disease are the same laws is an old maxim which few, if any, are disposed to doubt. The illustrations of my leading thought come with an equal abundance and impressiveness from the upper and the lower side of life. In little things or great the doctrine holds, To him that hath shall be given. On that ambrosial night when we saw Browning at home, and he showed us the veritable book out of which grew his marvellous poem "The Ring and the Book," he showed us other things that had been sent to him because the senders knew that they were things after his own heart,—a medal of his beloved pope, a contemporary picture of the execution of his wretched Guido Franceschini, and so on. Let a man have any dominant taste or sentiment or aspiration, and it becomes magnetic to the things that nourish it and give it power and scope. I have never forgotten a phrase in one of Mr. Staples's sermons,—he that flamed up where I am standing now, before I came. It was "a fate of good fellows." It was a fate of bad fellows that he meant; for the connection was: "Has a man chosen coarseness? His choice seems at once to embody itself in his companions, who become a fate and fury to him. .... How many a man becomes fixed in habits of indulgence in this way! Before he is aware of it, his indulgence, at first casual, gets organized into a fate of good fellows who almost force him to his ruin." But, whether good fellows or bad fellows, the law, the principle, is just the same. Given a prurient tendency, and what encouragement it gets from men and books! As for the latter, they seem to shape themselves from out the circumambient air; and those that the clean-minded find innocent enough yield to the baser sort some contribution to their stock in trade, something confirmatory of the fault with which they palter when they ought to strike it down. It is just so with any evil tendency. It is a principle of aggregation that is selective of the companions, the friends, the books, the studies, the circumstances, that will establish and entrench a man in a fortress almost impregnable to the assault of good or ill, according as the dominant, selective principle is one that makes for blessing or for bane.

And the upshot of the whole matter is, Beware! In the early Christian scriptures, not included in the New Testament, there are some pregnant sayings attributed to Jesus; and one of these, "Be ye good bankers," looks as if it might originally have been a part of the parable of the talents which I have read to you this morning, and from which my text was taken, "Be ye good bankers." That is to say, Knowing this universal tendency of life to aggre-

gate *about* a man and *in* a man such things as are according
to his dominant tendencies of mind and heart, beware what
you invest. Ask yourselves honestly, Is this or that something that I am willing and glad to have increase till it becomes my fate, my character, my life? For these are those
who, not having asked this question manfully, or having
failed to act according to the answer given, have gone on
from bad to worse until there has seemed to be for them no
place for repentance, though they have sought it diligently
and with tears. But if we would be good and true, helpful
and kind and brave, thank Heaven the world abounds in
men and books, in situations and events, with a celestial
ichor in their veins, which, if we choose, can be transfused
into our own, in order that thereby we may be strong for the
upholding of all honorable contentions and the beating of
all mean and hateful passions down.

THE POSSIBLE LIFE.

I HAVE had some very pleasant Sunday services in the course of my vacation, but only two or three of them have been of the conventional type. More frequently they have been of that kind the robins and the thrushes institute in their leafy choirs, and which has found in the most quaint of modern poets a felicitous interpretation, thus :—

> Some keep the Sabbath going to church:
>   I keep it staying at home,
> With a bobolink for chorister
>   And an orchard for a dome.
> Some keep the Sabbath in surplice;
>   But I just wear my wings,
> And instead of tolling the bell for church
>   My little sexton sings.
>
> God preaches,—a noted clergyman,—
>   And the sermon is never long.
> So instead of going to heaven at last,
>   I'm going all along.

One of our best of these out-of-door services was a few Sundays since. Stepping southward, we felt the wind blow as refreshingly upon our faces as if it came from its familiar western cave. And, as we went along, the fields new-mown, or with their scanty rowen softer for the foot, invited us continually to leave the beaten track, and try their possibilities of homely pleasantness. For all the bars were down, as if to say to us, Come in! come in! How could we choose but heed so sweet an invitation? So in we went upon the right hand and the left, and made such beautiful discoveries that we said how foolish we had been to come that way so often, and never turn aside before with vagrant feet to seek a newer world. The very rudeness of our mountain scene, the roughness of our meagre soil, made beauty for us as we went. The way of the transgressor may be hard in spiritual things, but in things natural I have ever found going across lots one of the most inspiriting and free and glad. What nooks and corners shadowed by the gigantic bowlders which the glaciers had brought down with them as they went crawling south! What lordly trees which by their proud magnificence had prevailed upon the thrifty farmer to withhold his axe, albeit conscious of a wealth of firewood lavishly foregone, and some armfuls of good hay diminished by the shade! In these seclusions, how far away, how non-existent, seemed the city's madding crowd, and even the village neighbor-hood!

> O peace and rest! upon the breast
>   Of God himself we seemed to lean;
> No break or bar of sun or star,
>   Just he and we, and naught between!

So many treasures did we find, belated blueberries, and small black cherries, tasting of our early prime,— what taste more sweet upon life's westering slope!— that straightway then and there it was highly resolved that in future we would make such ventures oftener, and see what riches we could find.

That day I found my sermon for this morning with the rest; and here it is,— a sermon of the possible life, the open doors, the bars let down, the frankest invitation to such travellers as you and I to leave the beaten tracks and try the neighboring fields. I know well enough how the sweet habitudes of our domestic life and our customary relations with each other in the round of social duties and amenities conserve much that is excellent. There has been a struggle for existence on these lines, as well as in the animal and vegetable worlds; and the established order is in no small degree the survival of the fittest. But, however it may be with the plant or animal in which fixity of type is everything and there is no tendency to variation, the social or domestic, the political or religious life that comes to this has reached the beginning of the end,— the end of growth, if not of mere existence, between which and death there is not much to choose. The conventional is a vampire that sucks out the life of individuals and institutions, slowly it may be, but with an insistence that is sure as the habitual alternations of the day and year. What can be more inane than is the formal interchange of social compliment among persons who make up what is called good "society"? And what can be more encouraging than the damage done to this by the more active intellectual and moral life of women, bringing them together in some earnest, vital way, and leaving them no time to waste on mere formalities?

Religion has no deadlier enemy than conventional acceptance of its creeds, and a similar observance of its forms. There is more religion in the deliberate atheism of some people than in the voluble assent of some others, because it corresponds to something real, because it means that the man is really thinking for himself, that he is really touched and moved, impassioned and tormented, by the insoluble problems of existence and the tragic aspects of the natural and social worlds. I have told you probably of an old-time minister in Marblehead who used to pray twice every Sunday for those who go down to the sea in ships,— "May they be blessed with a perpetual calm." *Dis aliter visum:* the old, weather-beaten skippers in the pews saw it quite otherwise. Now there are always people whose ideal of the perfect in religion is that of Parson Dana for his fisherman,— a perpetual calm. But the history of religion shows that its periods of vitality have been its periods of controversy, agitation, change. Some of our Unitarians are quite too easily troubled by a little difference of opinion between different sections of the body; and when a few years ago we had a love-feast at Saratoga, and wiped out our old preamble and began again, they thought that we had arrived at length to a definite, coherent homogeneity, and that we should never have any differences of opinion any more. We were to stop thinking, and just chant in unison, "Love to God and love to man; Love to God and love to man," till the millennial dawn. Some of you must remember how happily Mr. Crothers satirized this notion at one of our social meetings, telling the story of the preacher who demanded with such vociferous iteration, "Who would be a goat?" that at last a man in a back seat got up and announced that, as no one else seemed willing to officiate in that capacity, *he* would be a goat. So Mr. Crothers told us that, so necessary was it to have some honest difference of opinion for the health of our religious body, that, if nobody else was ready to start in with some novel bit of heresy or schism, he would offer himself in that capacity. "Not as if I had already attained," said the apostle; and some of us, I know, have wondered whether a certain flatness, which has succeeded to our previous exaltation has not resulted from our thinking that we had already attained, and would be no more troubled with the void and pang of unfulfilled desire.

All this is episodical, and has perhaps kept me too long from the main stream of my discourse. But the lesson is extremely pertinent when so many mere apologists, masked as philosophers, argue with much plausibility that here and there evolution, to which of course they heartily subscribe, has done its best, and can no farther go. Christianity is its consummate flower. If, yes, and perhaps! If so, it is a Christianity which has not yet seen the light, a Christianity of the future, not of any past. "Revolutions," said Victor Hugo, "never stop half-way." Evolution never stops anywhere. When it stops, it ceases to be evolution, and becomes arrested development. The race, the institution, the religion, having the promise of no further growth, enters upon a period of death in life, and slow, immitigable decay.

But I am more anxious to apply my doctrine of the open doors, the invitations of fresh opportunities from the beaten tracks, to our individual experience than to that of any social aggregates, religious or political. Those of you who have read the life of Dr. Holmes must have had a kind of shiver at the thought what a mere accident it was that revealed to him that power the genial exercise of which made him an autocrat to whose rule we have subjected ourselves with great joy and gladness; and the shiver has been more searching of our joints and marrow when we have thought of Abraham Lincoln, how, but for the contest with Douglas, which gave the world assurance of a man, he might have been merely a long-limbed, story-telling circuit lawyer all his days; or of Grant that, but for the war's great opportunity to prove himself, he might have sunk in a few years into that drunkard's grave toward which in 1861 his feet were set upon a sharp incline. Here for a moment let me pause to say that such things should encourage us most pleasantly, when our good Ship of State seems to be drifting on a shore that ominously roars as if it hungered for its prey. Where are the men, we say, to lead us now as we were led before? And you will hear some talking as if

> Once to every man and nation
>   Comes the moment to decide,
> In the strife of truth with falsehood,
>   For the good or evil side,

and as if that once were now, and. choosing wrongly, we should float forevermore a derelict among the nations of the earth or go to pieces on the jagged rocks. These doleful prophecies are gross exaggerations of a trouble that is real enough. For, if we make some terrible mistake, through the swift misery and destruction it will bring upon us we shall find out how foolish we have been, and seek the better way; and in the day of our distress men will emerge from deep obscurity equal to the event, whatever it may be. No one had a classified list of the men who brought us through the red sea of the Civil War in advance of that momentous time. Fame does not sound a trumpet before her, as the hypocrites do in the synagogues and at the corners of the streets. She can keep her secrets, as we common mortals seldom can or do. The shore of time is strewn with nations

that have gone to wreck.   It is like that "ocean graveyard,"
as they call Sable Island, where so many ships lie buried in
the sand.   But there would be ten to one, if not an hundred, if all the prophecies of doom which timorous and coward hearts have spoken had been fulfilled.   If America can
be ruined by a financial blunder of the East or the West, she
does not deserve the sacrifices that have been made for her ;
and, the sooner History blots out her name, the better for
mankind.

But what I had in mind when I spoke of Dr. Holmes's
glad self-revelation and of those continental men which
Lincoln and Grant discovered in themselves, when all the
winds were loose, was that, however special their experience,
it hints at the fact that even the most ordinary lives run
parallel with splendid opportunities,— splendid, that is, compared with the habitual life with which we are contented, if
not satisfied.   Of all Philip Gilbert Hamerton's books the
most delightful has ever been to me "The Unknown River,"
the book itself too generally, I find, unknown.   Now, by
"The Unknown River" he does not mean any river which
has not heretofore been discovered or set down upon the
maps.   He means a river by whose banks men had built
their houses, and in whose rippling waters women had
washed their clothes, and boys and girls had dabbled with
untroubled joy, but of whose possibilities of gleam and
gloom, of fitful wandering, of infinite beauty of one kind
and another, all these had been as unconscious as if no
such river had ever stolen, with shy whispers and low laughter, through their sunlit fields or given them back from its
unruffled breast the light of moon and stars.   Oh, there are
many unknown rivers in the world, and unknown mountains,
too, and hills and glades and woodland solitudes,— unknown or known but to a few, and known in various degrees.   I think, sometimes, that I know pretty well our
Hampshire County woods and waters.   But if John Bur-
roughs or my friend William Hamilton Gibson, with whom I
shall have pleasant speech no more, could have had my

twenty years among them, what blankest ignorance would my knowledge be compared with theirs !

All this is parable of spiritual realities. There is a river the streams whereof make glad or sad the places where we live and love and have our joy and sorrow,—the river of life, of your individual life and mine. And it is for the most of us an unknown river, or known so dubiously and imperfectly that our knowledge in comparison with what it might and ought to be is hardly worthy of the name.

> Perhaps in us all there are heights of will
> And shadowy deeps of thought,
> A land in the heart of each one's life
> With self-surprises fraught.

Why do we say "perhaps," when every one of us at times has had some "intimation clear of wider scope," of "larger life upon our own impinging"? Nay, but it is our own, only unrecognized commonly as such, unclaimed or unreclaimed, left for chance growths of thought and will to thrive upon, when we might make it laugh with the abundance of its cheer. The surprises of genius, the awakening of great writers and captains and statesmen to undreamed of possibilities in their own natures, are but the signs and pledges of the outlying powers and graces that surround the actual accomplishment of the most ordinary men and women. These, too, have their surprises, "when their passions seem to speak for them, and they only to stand by and wonder," as George Eliot has written, and not only, as her special instances suggest, their evil passions, but their passions of heroism and fidelity, of devotion and self-sacrifice, of sublime nobility, where they themselves and those who know them best imagine no such possibilities. We have had a literature of such things during the last twenty years, a better comment than our liberal theology on the old dogma of total depravity, revealing as it does the beneficent and god-like forces that are masked by faces dull with the moral inertia of a life unvisited by soft persuasion or by strong appeal, or brutalized with the experience of private shame or others' curse and ban. Are these stories, do you imagine, an exaggeration of the better side of human nature, so different from the obverse which it presents to our habitual knowledge and regard? I have not thought them so. Rather have I thought that the surprises of genius, wonderful as they are, are not so wonderful as the surprises that are hidden in the most unfeatured or disfeatured lives that make up the majority of those which constitute our personal environment from year to year. And my happy confidence that this is so is no mere wilful optimism, but an inference entirely logical from the things I know to those beyond my ken. So splendid are the revelations of nobility in the sphere of our habitual knowledge that we are bound both to imagine and believe that the dark we cannot see is starred all over with like admirable instances of things bravely done and sweetly borne and loftily withstood for truth and righteousness.

And yet, and yet,— is not the wonder this, not that there are so many of these revelations which assure us of a multitude beyond our personal horizon, but that with such good and great things possible, and so often actualized, our average life keeps so persistently the beaten tracks of thought and will, so seldom ventures to explore the possibilities that lie, it may be, only a little way off from these? Alike our physiology and our psychology, as now developed, make plain as possible that people generally are living on the thinnest outer crust of their capacity. There is something infinitely suggestive in the things done for a Laura Bridgman or a Helen Keller and their family of pitiable souls, in the persistency with which science, love, and patience have stormed all the shut gates of sense until the siege is raised, and those within the sevenfold bars find themselves in glad communication with the outer world and with the friends who have so wrought for their release. But, within the range of normal sensibility and physical condition, we are hardly less impressed with the wide reach of the outlying possibility. We demur at Plotinus because he was ashamed of his body. But have not the most of us good reason to be so, when over against our sickly flabbiness we see the athlete's muscles hard as iron, the dancer's supple as a Damascus blade? Consider, too, what patience and persistency can do with that marvellous instrument, the human voice. You will say, perhaps, that we are not all professional singers, and cannot devote years of painful labor to the development of our vocal cords. True, very true; but, if the singer's patience can achieve so much, why, asks Professor Hiram Corson, who is a master in this sphere, should not thousands of men and women have some use of their voices, some skill in reading or in conversation that would add no trifling increment to the pleasantness of human life? For then a pleasant voice, or one well used, would not be so rare a thing as to fairly startle us with its divine surprise.

And still I talk in parables; but these last considerations bring me home to what has been from first to last my central thought,— the wealth of our outlying possibilities of use and joy. This is my argument : If patience and persistency, wisely directed, can enable the blind to see, the deaf to hear, the dumb to speak, or at least give them something corresponding to each normal sense, vastly delimiting the bounded sphere of their original condition, what might not a tithe of such patience and persistency do for the man of normal sensibility? Hardly should we exaggerate if we said that it might do as much for him as all the skill of Dr. Samuel G. Howe did for the objects of his supreme devotion and his patient skill. Hardly should we exaggerate if we said that there is all the difference between the actual and possible world of the average man or woman that there is between the deaf and dumb and sightless world and that which science and devotion give to those who wander aimlessly in such a world, most miserable to see. These things are true upon the physical plane. They are true of man's whole bodily constitution in the range of all its powers and gifts. And they are not less true of all the higher ranges of his life, if, indeed, there is a higher and a lower in an organism in which every part has its consenting function to perform, in which every part is implicated in the play of all the rest. I know how some of you have thrilled all through with perfect joy when reading that part of the engineer's story, as told by Rudyard Kipling, which describes the engine in the ocean steamer's hold : —

" Lord, send a man like Robbie Burns to sing the song o' steam !
  To match wi' Scotia's noblest speech yon orchestra sublime,
  Whaurto, uplifted like the just, the tail-rods mark the time.
  The crank-throws give the double-bass ; the feed-pump sobs and
    heaves :
  And now the main eccentrics start their quarrel on the sheaves.
  Her time, her own appointed time, the rocking link-head bides,
  Till — hear that note ?— the rod's return whings glimmerin' thro' the
    guides.
  They're all awa'! True beat, full power, the clanging chorus goes
  Clear to the tunnel where they sit, my purrin' dynamoes.
  Interdependence absolute, foreseen, ordained, decreed
  To work, ye'll note, at any tilt and every rate of speed.
  Fra sky-lift to furnace-bars backed, bolted, braced, and stayed,
  An' singin' like the mornin' stars for joy that they are made."

It seems we *have* a man like Robbie Burns to sing the song of steam. And now God send another such to sing the song of man ! Think you that, rightly sung, it would not be a higher and a deeper song than this of the great engine, throbbing and panting in the ocean steamer's hold, a grander song than that ? For there is no such piece of work as man in the consenting unity of all his physical and intellectual and moral powers. And, as Robert Fulton's first invention was to the Cunarder of our time,— with the power of seven thousand horses active in her machinery,— so are the majority of men and women, in their various ineptitude of body, mind, and heart, in comparison with the possible development of these that waits for them beyond the verge of their accustomed life and never far away.

Such is our case that both the surprises of power and goodness in great and little men, and the slow strenuousness and rich rewards of long endeavor after this or that ideal excellence, assure us of our infinite reserves of various power and use. Here are the roadside fields wherein I found the hint of my discourse that pleasant Sunday morning. What was their utmost mystery and charm compared with the immeasurable satisfactions and delights that constantly impinge upon our daily walk! But the open gates, the bars let down, the frank and pleasant invitations to forsake the travelled road and try the springy turf, the homely cheerfulness, the sweet seclusions of the fields,— where do I find things parallel to these in our habitual experience of intellectual and spiritual things? Where do we not find them, rather? For it is not as if the good of life were in the main a matter either of those moments which surprise and startle us into a nobler life or of those strenuous endeavors whereby men brace their faculties to deeds of daring excellence. These grand surprises and these strenuous endeavors give us the measure of our possibilities. They apprize us of "the man beyond man," whose beatific vision and whose high behavior shame our average works and days. They are a portion and an inheritance for which we may indeed be grateful and of which we may well be proud. But, thank Heaven, our dependence for the average good of life and for its constant betterment is not on these divine surprises nor upon these strenuous endeavors. The "fee simple" in which we hold this good and betterment is much simpler than it would be if we were so conditioned. It is the frank and pleasant invitation which is extended to us every day and hour to venture on some noble enterprise of thought or will. Here the open door is a good book, a better book than we are commonly contented with, — a book to make us think, a book that may require some bracing of the mind in order to be successfully encountered. Here it is an opportunity to perform some act of kindness, just to say a kind word, perhaps, where it would do some good, or to withhold an unkind word where it would hurt and harm. Again, it is some full exposure of our minds to some novel system of ideas, something that affronts all of our prejudices and preconceptions, but no less on that account may be a higher truth than we have known. What we want is a habit of open-minded approach to the unhabitual in thought and life, so that life may keep its freshness for us, and not degenerate into mere humdrum or routine. And, once we can establish such a habit of cordial welcome to the unhabitual, we shall find that the opportunities to practise it are not infrequent or remote.

Fixity of type and a tendency to variation are the poles between which the evolution of the planet swings secure, and that of all its myriad forms; and the same poles appear, or should appear, in every individual life. There must be stability with variation, or a man will be carried about by every wind of doctrine, by every impulse of his personal and social life. So, too, we must be on our guard lest the new thing that is offered us is not some old and outworn principle or creed. Our social markets, political and religious, abound in panaceas that have been tried and found wanting; and the mirage which is so tempting to the reformer often lights the way to "that Serbonian bog where armies whole have sunk."

But take my thought in its simplicity. It is not, I trust, a bad one for the beginning of another year. It is first the fulness and the richness of the possibilities that lie just beyond the average round of our experience. It is next that these, however they may be assured to us by the surprises of power and genius or by the strenuous fidelities of much-enduring men, are not exhausted by these exceptional examples, but plead with us at doors that open out from the activities of the most ordinary lives, wherever there is thought to think, or help to give, or choice is proffered between less and greater things. Life's countless leasts mount up to larger sums of truth and good than its great moments of heroic energy and daring will. But it is true, as Emerson has written, that difficult duty is never far off; and it is also true that the most difficult, yet most inescapable, is frequently a door that opens for us into some treasure-house of our own being, some better appreciation of our social opportunities, some closer access to the patient heart of God.

THE HOUSE OF PAIN.

What a great House it is! And the rooms in it, how
many! They say there are eleven thousand in the Vatican;
but there are more in this. Those in the Vatican are great
and small; so these. There is the Armenian room, "a sym-
phony in red" for Mr. Whistler's daring hand, one monstrous
flow of crimson everywhere, one hundred thousand men,
women, and children slaughtered horribly. We think that
we are getting on. What splendid things the poets say
about the day before us and the night behind! But how
far back must we go to find a chapter of horrors in the book
of history that is so terrible as this? And we hardly think
of it. The great powers of Europe that might by their con-
certed action put a stop to all this devilry without the firing
of a gun are paralyzed by mutual jealousies; and the Sultan
goes his way dancing, how gracefully, along an ever widening
stream of blood and tears. How little do we realize the
meaning of these things! If they only meant so many mur-
dered, so many killed outright, it wouldn't be so bad. But
the intolerable fear, the homeless wandering, the sufferings
and horrors worse than death,— these make the Armenian
room in the great House of Pain something to make our
breathing hard, something to stop the heart, or would if we
were not so powerless to imagine what we cannot see. And
then, too, we are much engrossed by the sad condition of
our own farming population,— so many millions of them
starving; not actually, but in the rhetorical exaggeration of
the political stump orator and the party press.

This great Armenian room is not at our end of the house.
There is another one that is,— the Cuban room. This, too, is
furnished in crimson, like the other. But it is not so bad as
that. In Cuba the insurrectionists are making such a fight
for independence as puts the heroisms of our literature of

blood and iron, so popular at present, quite to shame.
These, too, will have their novelists some day, and then
men's blood will quicken or will freeze to think of such
things done and suffered. Moreover, the Spanish soldiers
are something different from the Turkish murderers.
Whether they know or not that some one has blundered,

> "Theirs not to make reply,
> Theirs not to reason why,
> Theirs but to do and die."

And if they are not doing much to quell the insurrection,
they are dying fast enough,—faster of fever than by sword
and shot. And how meagre is our realization of what is
going on in this one room of the great House of Pain! For
us the twenty thousand young men of the Spanish army who
have perished in this monstrous struggle are merely so many
Spanish soldiers. But in reality they are so many brothers,
lovers, husbands, sons,— loved, cherished, missed, and
mourned as tenderly as those whom we sent up to battle
in our times that tried men's souls. Here is another scandal
of our civilization,— that there should be no comity of nations that can prevail to stay this awful strife. "All men
become good creatures," sings the poet, "but so slow." Ah,
yes, indeed, so very, very slow.

Many of those eleven thousand rooms in the Vatican must
be very little rooms, and the meanest of them are probably
much finer than some of the smallest in the House of Pain.
What impresses us is the big rooms like those we have been
visiting, and the earthquake room, the tornado room, the
inundation room, in all of which, however, the destruction of
life is not the most tragic incident. But in reality there is
always more suffering going on in the smallest rooms of this
sad house than in the largest ones. Why but because they
are so many, though each had, as so many have, only a
single sufferer. The great railway accident which destroys
a score or two of lives sends a great shudder through the
whole community: but in 1893 there were 2,727 employés
killed on the railroads of the United States, 31,729 injured

more or less cruelly. One employé was killed of every 320 men; one injured in every 28. Now, if we could follow up each one of these fatalities into the family, the home, on which it fell, what an amount of suffering, physical or mental, would be brought into our ken, what broken fortunes, broken limbs, and broken hearts! Yet what an infinitesimal fraction it would be of all the suffering the sun and stars look down upon at any given time! I have spoken of the physical, so far, almost exclusively, or of that which has some physical cause. But how small a part is this of the great sum! Another part is furnished by the reverses of fortune or the hopeless struggle against odds, another by the more hopeless struggle with some strong temptation, some besetting sin; and if you would see the veriest torture-chambers in the House of Pain you must go into those soli-tary rooms, some of them beautiful with the loveliest things the artist can devise, where there are men and women who have had their trust most shamefully abused or who have themselves abused the trust of others in some shameful way.

Old is this house of which I tell. Our oldest houses in America, even those of the Aztecs and the cliff-dwellers, are affairs of yesterday compared with this. We have writings thousands of years old which make it plain enough that in that far-off time this "house of many mansions" was already builded huge and strong, but these writings seem like modern literature when we think of the ages of suffering before they were written. For centuries and milleniums before the coming of man their endless corridors recede. The words of the apostles did not exceed the fact: "The whole creation groaneth and travaileth in pain together until now."

Of all the ancient books that made some brave attempt to grapple with the problem of suffering, the grandest and the noblest is the Book of Job. It has had much conventional admiration accorded it as a part of the Bible; but, if it could be discovered now for the first time, what an outburst of gen-uine admiration there would be! "There is a book for you!" the anti-Bible folk would say. "Nothing in your

Bible to compare with it." Time was when it was piously imagined to be the oldest book in the Old Testament, written long before Moses wrote the Pentateuch. The argument was a very simple and ingenuous one : The book was about the patriarch Job; therefore some patriarch must have written it,—probably Job himself. Who else could know so much about his personal affairs, and give such verbatim reports of his own speeches and those of his three friends, and Elihu and the Almighty? Our later criticism makes out the book to be one of the latest in the Old Testament canon. Like the cathedrals of the Middle Ages, which still fill the eye and heart with joy unspeakable, it was centuries in the making, and, like those, its different parts are different in their style. In some of the cathedrals you will find a Norman crypt, and then an early-pointed choir, a decorated transept, and a nave with the flat-roof and characteristic traceries of the perpendicular period. In the Book of Job there are as many styles of thought as there are styles of architecture in such a century-growing pile as that. First came the prologue and the epilogue ; and their teaching was that, if the good man suffered (and the whole book is restricted to the problem of the good man's suffering), it was only for a time. In the epilogue Job gets back all that he loses in the prologue, and something to reward him for his sufferings into the bargain. This was the Jewish way of looking at the matter for many hundred years. No suffering, it argued, but as the punishment of sin. If good men suffered, it was because their goodness was not genuine or complete. This was the doctrine of the three friends of Job in the dialogue which makes up the body of the book. Those miserable comforters insisted to his face that he must be a bad man, or he could not be so unfortunate ; and he as strenuously denied their allegations. In his denial we find the purpose of the dialogue which is *par excellence* the Book of Job. The three comforters all harp on the same thing ; but Job does not budge a jot from his conviction that he is a righteous man. We have still another explanation of the problem in the speech of Elihu. Evidently, we have in this speech an afterthought and an interpolation. This is made plain by the fact that, after he has got through, the book goes on just as if he had not spoken. What follows his speech harks back to what goes before it, and its omission simply closes up the ranks. The writer of this speech of Elihu plainly thought he could improve upon the speeches of Eliphaz and Bildad and Zophar. His improvement was that Job's sufferings were not meant for punishment, but for purification. "As gold is tried in the fire, so men are tried in the furnace of adversity." These are the words of another book, "The Wisdom of Solomon"; but they express the thought of Elihu quite perfectly. We have another solution in the speeches of Jehovah. It is that there is nothing for the good man suffering but to submit; as Thackeray said,

> To bow before the awful will, *
> And bear it with an honest heart,

without trying to explain it, or to understand why it is so.

These various solutions of the problem of suffering, and particularly the suffering of the good man,—although they are from two thousand to twenty-five hundred years old,— are still worth considering. Each one of them contains an element of truth, if no one of them is wholly satisfactory. Job's comforters were partly right in their contention that the presence of suffering argues something wrong in the man who suffers. It is a very dangerous doctrine which we often hear proclaimed, that success in business or in any field of enterprise or thought is more likely to attend the dishonest than the honest man. There are too many facts that lend themselves to the support of this doctrine. Nevertheless, in the long run and the wide sweep, the evidence is overwhelmingly in favor of honesty as the best policy,— as indeed it would be if it brought only ruin in its train. Most commonly, where business honesty is the precursor of misfortune, the honesty is not to blame, but some defect of insight or foresight, or the dishonesty of others. Given first-rate abilities, and first-rate character will be no handicap in the race for mercantile or political success.

One of the biggest chambers in the House of Pain is that
occupied by those whose sufferings are the result of accident.
We call it accident; but how much of it is something else?
Take the 2,700 deaths of railroad employés in a year, the
31,000 injuries, was there no "contributive negligence," as
they call it, think you, in all these, or were the most of
them on that account? The amount of suffering is enormous, which need not have been if men had done what
they knew well enough to be the fit, the sensible, the honorable thing. The old Jewish doctrine of material success
proportioned to the amount of character was not a doctrine
which fitted close to every personal experience. Job did
well to resent its application to himself; and, speaking as
he did, his words were spoken that the thoughts of many
hearts might be revealed. Nevertheless, a great deal of
suffering comes unquestionably from doing wrong; and before we "curse God and die," or curse our neighbors or
our fate, we had better ask ourselves what we have done to
bring ourselves to such a low estate. Better, far better, that
we should revert to the old Jewish doctrine — so much character, so much success — than teach our boys and our young
men that character has nothing to do with success, and that
the rewards of business and politics are for the tricksters
and the knaves. Surely it is not so.

Those who affirm the integrity of the Book of Job,— *i. e.,*
that all its parts belong to it just as they stand,— are obliged
to admit that the contribution of Elihu to the discussion is
passed over by Job and the Almighty with something less
than that "comparative respect which means the absolute
scorn." But it does not deserve to be treated so contemptu-
ously. It is a better contribution than Jehovah makes himself. As gold is tried in the fire, so men *are* tried in the furnace of adversity. We may be slow to say that suffering is
intended as the school of virtue, and we are very sure that it
is not always a successful one; but that many thousands, aye,
many millions, have from this nettle of disaster plucked the
flower of character, how can we doubt who within the narrow

range of our own observation have seen men doing it so
many times? Even "calamity falling on a base mind" does
not always harden it. Sometimes and often it turns men
from their evil ways. Sweet are the uses of adversity, as you
and I have often seen them working in one chamber or
another of the many-chambered House of Pain. We have
known men and women whose characters were steadily deteriorating in the glow of health, the sunshine of prosperity,
but who have become kinder, gentler, every way more lov-
able, under the stress of disappointment and anxiety and loss
and pain. Especially we have known that hardening of
men's disposition, of women's equally, which so often comes
with the long tide of happy, prosperous years, to be so
changed by sorrow and misfortune that it was just as if a
rock in the fierce sunshine should become a sod of violets.
And where the original tendency was to the higher things,
what ineffable beauty and sweetness have we not seen bud-
ding and blossoming under the stress of storms that should,
it would seem, have crushed the stoutest heart?

Unquestionably, Jehovah's part of the discussion represents the opinion of the main author of the Book of Job, the
author of the great debate between Job and his three friends.
He would not have put into the mouth of Jehovah a solution
which did not seem to him superior to all the others and
which was not the best he had himself to give. And what
was this solution? That God did a thousand things Job
could not understand. Why then should he hope to understand the mystery of his own suffering? You all know, I
trust, the passage, the most magnificent in the Old Testament,
if not in any literature, in which Jehovah makes a recital of
his wondrous works and crushes Job under the weight of
his own feebleness in comparison with the Almighty and his
ignorance of the Almighty's ways. Here is really no solution at all, and it has not been accepted as one by the earnest thinkers of the world. Job might lay his hand upon his
mouth; these have declined to follow his example. Shall
the clay say unto the potter, Why hast thou made me thus?

Yea, verily it shall, or prove itself a vessel of dishonor. But if the answer of Jehovah out of the whirlwind was no answer, there was in it the suggestion of a helpful one. If man's ignorance of the universe may not crush him down into abject submission, his knowledge of it may enable him to trust the Power which manifests itself in its sublime order and beauty and beneficence. The modern Job *can* answer a great many of the questions which the man of Uz found altogther answerless. And from his answers he derives a noble confidence in that power as the sufficient guardian of our human life. Theologians have always made a great virtue of trusting where we are blindly ignorant. But there is no virtue in such trusting. Ignorance as such is no ground for trust whatever. But when we know in part and what we know is good, then we may rationally trust in good beyond our ken.

One thing is sure : Jehovah's answer out of the whirlwind did not make an end of the discussion. It has been going on from the time when Job fell silent until now. Never was it more active than at the present time. The several answers of the book of Job have constantly recurred, more or less varied in their form. We have had some insisting on the doctrine of Job's comforters, that all suffering is the punishment of sin ; some on his stout denial of that doctrine ; some taking up the parable of Elihu, and pleading for the disciplinary and redeeming quality of pain ; and some, also, endeavoring, after the manner of Jehovah in the old Hebrew drama, to crush us down into abject submission, because we are so little and the Almighty is so great ; because we know so little, and he knows so much.

It would manifestly be impossible for me to enter into a detailed account of the different forms these different doctrines have assumed, or of the multitude of other theories which have from time to time been broached. The most popular in Christendom has been the silliest of all,— that Adam and Eve, by eating the forbidden fruit in Eden, "brought sin into the world, and all our woes." Within

fifty years we have had scholars of great reputation teaching
sincerely, or at least without the Roman augur's grin satiri-
cal, that the suffering of the animal world for ages before
Adam was anticipatory of his fall and was the imputed punishment thereof. Such stuff as this still furnishes harmless
amusement to a few isolated minds; but the great tides of
modern thought have left them high and dry, braiding their
ropes of sand with great self-satisfaction. But if we may not
consider separately the multitude of theories which have
been brought into existence to account for the House of
Pain and the innumerable tragedies that are enacted in its
innumerable rooms, we can at least distinguish a few tendencies of thought which rise from out the multitude of
explanations,— as from the long line of the Alps you see
rise into loftier air, as you look southward from the Rigi's
top, the Wetterhorn, the Silberhorn, the Jungfrau, and other
dark or shining peaks.

We have first, then, the tendency of optimistic evolution,
This is pre-eminently the tendency of liberal theologians
who have taken up with the doctrine of evolution. These
allow the reality of the House of Pain; but they insist that
it is only a prison and a hospital on its way to be a palace,— a
people's palace, with every convenience and enjoyment that
can be desired. All pain and suffering and sin, they tell us,
are simply maladjustment: the organization and the environment are out of gear with each other, and they consequently
create friction; and that means suffering and sin. There is
much here that is worth considering. Evidently a world
a-making should not be judged as if it were already made.
As well might we have judged our Brooklyn Bridge when
only the foot-walk was swung across, and said, "What a
miserable bridge!" But there are many aspects of the
problem of suffering which this optimistic evolution does
not seem to touch; and not only so, but there are many
aspects of evolution which do not seem to help this optimistic scheme of thought. At any rate, we have our pessimistic
evolutionists as well as our optimistic evolutionists; and they

are many.   Moreover, they are oftenest found, I think,
among the teachers of pure science,— men who go to Nature
simply to find out her secrets, and not among the theologians
who too often go to her with a preconceived opinion for
which they ingeniously seek her confirmation.   These men of
science march with Huxley, and with him find the cosmos
anti-ethical and full of pain.   But some of them have Huxley's courage, and believe that, if man against the universe
cannot do everything, he can still do much.   This is the
temper of the pessimistic evolutionist when he is at his best ;
and he is not the worst fellow in the world to have round.

Next we have the tendency of the religious optimist.
From first to last we have had much of this tendency.   It is
not a bad tendency for good people ; it is not a good tendency for bad people.   It suggests too pointedly that they
should continue in sin that grace may abound.   In its confidence that all is for the best, it is in danger of becoming, as
Professor Royce has shown, " out and out immoral."   It
denies squarely that there is any House of Pain.   Those
who imagine they have seen it towering high up against the
sky and shutting out the sun, have been the victims of an
illusion.   Those who imagine they have wandered through
its endless wards, or that they have themselves suffered in
them grievously, have equally been the victims of an illusion.
The corollaries of these propositions should, it would seem,
be evident enough.   If sin is an illusion, why should we not
sin?   "If all is well, what is there to resist, to conquer, to
meet courageously, to regret, to avoid? . . . If divine wisdom
is equally present in the highest and the lowest, equally in
the good and the ill, why then resist the unreal evil?" *   If,
as Emerson has written of God,

> " Alike to him the better, the worse,
>   The glowing angel, the outcast corse,"

why should we be so careful to discriminate ?

* Royce's " Spirit of Modern Philosophy " (p. 440).   The whole chapter is the most
inspiring treatment of my subject that I know, as my liberal quotations from it would
make evident if I withheld this grateful recognition.

There is another tendency which so much resembles this that it is frequently confounded with it; and indeed the average man cannot be expected to distinguish one of these tendencies from the other. Do not imagine that, in describing the one or the other, I am simply describing covertly the Christian Science doctrine of our time. This, as it comes within the range of my attention, is not careful to discriminate between the religious optimism I have described and the religious mysticism which finds in pain only absorption in our own finitude, and for its cure commands absorption in the contemplation of God's infinite perfection. There is, there can be, we are assured with endless iteration, no imperfection and no pain in God, and whoso dwelleth in God, dwelleth in painlessness and perfect peace. To whichever of these tendencies the Christian Science of our time is most allied, it is no parvenu, no new-comer in philosophy or religion; it is but the recrudescence of a doctrine which has had as many positively last appearances as a famous actor, who is always sure of coming back. With its practical efficiency I have no present concern. That is a matter of psychology; and all that is claimed for it may be entirely sure, and still the religious theory of it be utterly unsound. Leaving the friends of Christian Science to decide to which of the two tendencies that I have last described their own doctrine is allied most closely, I hasten to say that whatever sanctities and beatitudes may be associated with the optimism that denies the existence of evil, and the mysticism which allows its reality only to our finite apprehension, "the two views" — as Prof. Royce has plainly shown — "agree in this: that they both deprive the finite world of all reality and of all deeper ethical significance. What we do here, he says, — our work, our purposes, our problems, our doubts, our battles, all these things have for the mystic as for the religious optimist no essential meaning. There are no issues in the finite world for either view. And this idea that, just because there are no issues in the finite world, just because there is no gravity about it, nothing stern, nothing worthy of a good fight, no salvation that may be lost and is hard to win, no significant toil that ought to be entered on, and that is calling for us with the voice of a positive duty,—what is such an idea but the very essence of pessimism itself?"

I am bound to say that I for one agree with this most heartily. I do not know of any sadder pessimism than that which denies the reality of the fight in which we are engaged. I am far enough from holding every theoretic optimist and mystic to the logical significance of their belief. "Gray is all theory," said Goethe, "and green the glittering tree of life." Theorize as they may, good earnest men and women will act as if the poet's "Life is real, life is earnest" had divine meaning for us yet, as if the House of Pain were not something non-existent or man's shadow on the void of heaven, but something as substantial as the pyramids or the Matterhorn; which, too, shall pass away. But it is always a great pity when our real life is at variance with our theory of life, when it is only through the seams and fractures in our logic that we see the face of God and the men and women who require our love and care.

There is an optimism which believes that we can reconcile the facts of life, however hard, with confidence in the Eternal Goodness. "Were it a problem," it tells us, "how to have a better world," that Goodness "would have solved the problem." "Were it a question of a wise choice," that Goodness "would have executed from eternity this wiser choice." "Were it a matter of foreign necessity that inflicted evil," that Goodness "would in existing have eternally absorbed this foreign element into his own organic nature. The world is then indeed, as Leibnitz said, the best of all possible worlds." " Yet one who finds himself," says the great teacher * who has argued thus and who has gone nearer then any one else, to my thinking, to the heart of this great matter,— " Yet one who finds himself close, as it were, to the gates of the celestial city and to a glimpse of the golden glories within it, nigh to the palace of the king,

---

* Professor Josiah Royce, Harvard University.

does, after all, well to tremble nevertheless, when he con-
siders how easy it is to say such things about the perfection
of God's world and how hard it is to give concreteness and
weight to the mere abstractions of the religious consciousness." And why? Because here is the House of Pain, no
unreality, no mere projection of ourselves upon the void,
but as real as anything can be, a terrible reality. How can
it be so real if God is infinite perfection and all things are
in God? That is a question to which I believe, if I had
time, and following reverently another's careful feet, I might
give some satisfactory reply. One thing is sure, if man is in
any real sense the measure of things, seeing that without a
real fight with evil his manhood could not be complete, a
world debarring us from the possibility of this fight would
not be a perfect world, nor the God creating it a perfect
God. But the near end is always best in studying God or
man. Better a thousand times deny the infinite perfection
than not to feel that, however it can be so, the House of
Pain is a reality, our fight with suffering and sin is just as
real as anything can possibly be. For how can we fight a
good fight if we believe our enemies a phantom horde?
We know that they are not. If we have the toothache we
have the toothache, and we are not going to lie about it,
even if by so doing we can reduce the pain. As here, so
everywhere. The great teacher whom I have been following
so eagerly assures us that without suffering, his own suffering, God could not be a perfect God.* Nevertheless, even
at the risk of fighting against God, we will do all that in us
lies to make the burden of man's pain lie lighter on his heart.
There will still be enough left for God's perfection, let us
hope. Or what if the good of pain and evil, for him as for
ourselves, consists in there being something for him to conquer,— the crown of his perfection, as of ours, the conquering
of these? However this may be, suffering exists for us as
something to abate, something to destroy. Forget everything else that I have said this morning, if you cannot help
it, but do not forget this.

* This in a remarkable address before the recent Ministers' Institute, at Concord,
Mass.

> If I can keep one heart from breaking
> , Or ease one pain,
> Or help one fainting robin
> Into its nest again,
> I shall not live in vain.

Less so than if with boundless confidence in the infinite perfection I stood lost in adoration before that, and in the mean time let slip some opportunity to help another's need, to cure another's hurt, to comfort another's sorrow, to forgive another's sin. I do believe that there is a divine philosophy which can reconcile the reality of evil with the perfection of the Eternal Goodness. Happy are they who can attain to this and hold it fast through every evil time! But life is more than theory; and the one thing needful is for us to believe in the reality of pain, the reality of evil, the reality of sin, and the reality of our ability to cope with these, reduce their bulk and power, and from our tough resistence win for ourselves some truer manhood, some diviner womanhood, than we ever yet have earned. Better the rankest pessimism which goes resolutely about to make less the mountain of iniquity than the most cheerful optimism which is lost in adoration of the beatific vision while there is wasted opportunity on either hand. Great is the House of Pain; many the rooms therein; many the weary sufferers whose eyes watch for the morning. Theirs are no phantom miseries. God may be infinitely perfect; but their days are full of agony and strife and wrong. If happily we are not of these — yet, who of us is not, at one time or another? — our part (and nothing can be plainer) is to do something, much if we can, and little if it must be so, for the abatement of their misery and pain. Trust me, our least endeavor in this kind will more approve us loyal sons and daughters of the most high God than would the most enraptured contemplation of his infinite perfection while still we left undone the things that touch the windows of the House of Pain as with the brightness of his everlasting light, the warmth of his eternal love.

MORAL ATHLETICS.

My subject is not a novel one. A most distinguished
preacher made it quite his own some eighteen centuries ago.
He called himself the least of the apostles,—this Saul of
Tarsus, afterward called Paul; but men do not always take
their own measure rightly, and we think of him to-day as
overtopping all the rest. In speaking of the moral strifes
and wrestlings of mankind, he expressed himself so often in
the terms of the athletic games the Greeks delighted in so
much that we could easily believe he had at some time run
a race himself or tried a fall with some one in the Greco-
Roman city where he was born; or, if not this, that he had
no languid interest in the trials of speed and strength in
which other youth engaged.

You might say, possibly, that his subject was not so much
moral athletics in these passages as it was athletic morals;
and I should answer that my subject, too, is not so much
moral athletics as athletic morals. It is moral athletics in
the sense of athletic morals. But incidentally we have in
these sayings of the hero-saint something about moral athletics, something about the morals of athletics; as where
he says (or another in his spirit), "If a man strive for masteries, yet is he not crowned unless he strive lawfully."
There is an entering wedge; and, following it up, I could
easily enough split my discourse this morning into two parts,
—the first part about moral athletics, and the second part
about athletic morals. For the question of moral athletics,
the morals of athletics, is a much wider one than that which
the New Testament's "striving lawfully" suggests. That is
not unimportant; only, alas! it is not always true with us
that those who strive for masteries are not crowned unless
they strive lawfully. Literally, of course, our athletes are
not crowned at all; instead of the crown of wild olive which

the Greeks gave to their contestants, we give a medal or a cup. I am not sure that theirs was not the better way; and where our common and revised versions call that crown of wild olive a *corruptible* crown, remember that it means simply *perishable*, and always read it so. But this is by the way. What is more to the purpose is that sometimes in our contests those who contend unlawfully receive the prize. In our professional athletics this happens, I imagine, not unfrequently. It is arranged beforehand which side shall win, and so the betting is much more intelligent. At my only horse-race I saw a splendid creature sold out in this way; and then, mounted by a jockey who had never sat upon his back before, he, like Ben Adhem's name, "led all the rest." In the athletics of our college men such things are never done, but there has from time to time been much discussion as to whether the players have not deliberately, or in the ardor of the contest, exceeded the brutality which is unavoidable and is permitted them by the rules of the game. There was, you will remember, some two years ago, a very general feeling that "anything to win" was getting to be quite too much the order for the day; or that, if the game of foot-ball necessitated such brutalities as were in evidence, then it was not a game for gentlemen to be engaged in, nor one in which young men of honorable mind and decent character could engage without deteriorating to a lower plane.

But the morals of athletics is a much wider question than the New Testament "striving lawfully" either covers or suggests. It is not a question that I feel myself competent to discuss either in its narrower or wider implications. But certainly the amount of interest attaching to athletics in our universities and colleges and preparatory schools, as compared with that attaching to those studies for which these universities and colleges and schools were primarily intended, makes the broader question of the moral influence of athletics on our educated youth one of immense importance; and, quite as certainly, the incidents of death and mutilation which attend our school and college games should

give us pause upon the road which we are taking with such
eager haste. So far as the athletic tendency means a growing sense of the importance of a good physical foundation
for a man's culture and character it is most admirable. And
no one can admire more than I do the splendid pluck and
courage, and the magnificent energy and endurance, which
our young athletes exhibit on their various courses, tracks,
and fields. I am perhaps somewhat morbid in my admiration for these things, so painfully conscious am I of my own
miserable inefficiency upon the physical side, so horribly am
I cut off from even that fine indifference to wind and
weather which I see in others with a shamed and envious
heart.

> " God who created me
> Nimble and light of limb
> In three elements free —
> To run, to ride, to swim ;
> Not when the sense is dim,
> But now from the heart of joy
> I would remember him :
> Take the thanks of a boy."

That is a bit of poetry which I love to impress upon the
boys now growing up, though I can never recite it without a
pang of sorrow and regret and shame that I have been so
little free in two of the three elements my whole life long.

Yes, let us have the physical basis of culture and character. Let us have the strength and the endurance which
can only come through manly exercises on the cindered
path and the contentious field. And let us not make hypocrites of our young men by asking them to pretend that physical culture is their only motive in the matter. There is
also the *gaudium certaminis,*— the joy of battle. Man is a
competitive animal. Our socialists and communists imagine
that they can make him over into a purely co-operative one ;
but they never can or will. But one thing is sure : if our
athletics are not all for fun, if they have some justification
from the side of physical culture, we have a right to demand
of our young men that they shall not poison, with tobacco or

with drink or baser things, the blood which they have tried to sweeten, the strength which they have tried to harden, in their various sports.

One other thing is sure : that whatever value we may set on physical strength and courage and endurance, these things are not sufficient for the making of a man, and they are not sufficient to justify the splendid gifts which have been lavished on our schools and colleges by their various benefactors, from their foundation until the present time. To train men for the ministry and to educate the Indians were the two objects which the founders of Harvard College had in mind. One of these objects is about as far as the other from the hopes and purposes of those who are now interested in the welfare of the college. Lowell says that the Indians showed much greater aptitude for disfurnishing the outsides of other people's heads than for furnishing the insides of their own. But, if physical energy and endurance are the be-all and the end-all of a college course, what the Indians were at the beginning of the business is what the young collegiate of the athletic kind aspires to be upon the crowning height. Let us, by all means, have physical strength, courage, and endurance,— the more of these the better; but let us not have the emphasis which these things are getting in the popular and student mind blind us entirely to the fact that our schools and colleges are institutions of learning, devoted to "the humanities," the liberal arts, and that the young men who seek them mainly as a stage on which to show off their physical prowess are false to their most honorable traditions, and should betake themselves elsewhere.

Great is physical culture ; but it is not all. Indeed, we can conceive a man lacking it altogether, like Dr. Channing, whose social weight could not be measured by any number of foot-ball champions who are merely that. I have known women shut up in the house for years,— invalids, suffering much of pain, and more of deprivation,— the sum of whose enjoyments, intellectual and moral, the measure of whose spiritual significance, I would no more exchange for that of your physical giant, indifferent to intellectual and spiritual things, than I would exchange so much weight of gold or precious stones for an equal weight of dirt swept from the street. Let us have the physical energy and prowess, but let us also have "the things that are more excellent." And let us rejoice and be exceeding glad that the whole story of our collegiate life has not been told when some wit has said, in Byron's memorable phrase, " These are our young barbarians *all at play*." They are not *all* at play; and some of those who are, do not play all the time, but give themselves in fuller measure to those intellectual exercises and encounters by which the mind is braced for the great contests of the business or the political arena in which every educated man is honor-bound to take no sneaking part.

I am dwelling much longer than I meant to on this part of my discourse. You will begin to think it was suggested by the various rivalries which have adorned Thanksgiving week. But I had not thought of these as coming when I chose the subject some weeks in advance. They have, perhaps, detained me longer in the vestibule of my discourse than I should have stayed there but for their dominance in the social atmosphere we have all been breathing latterly. But now I come to the moral athletics which I had specially in mind when I said in my heart that upon this subject would I write. As I have said, perhaps Athletic Morals would be a better indication of the matter which I am meaning to bring home to you with such clearness and such cogency as I can command. It is this matter : That we do not lack for opportunities in our personal and social life for something as athletic for the mind and will as are the physical contests of the time for those who are engaged in them ; that all the " good courages " are not confined to such contests, and were not exhausted by the military ardors of the race ; nor are they to be looked for only where these still have full scope. Nothing is surer than that a love of danger and of daring is a factor inseparable from the constitution of the race. It is not the sea, as Emerson has sung, that makes

" Some coast alluring, some lone isle,
To distant men who must go there or die,"—

who must go there whether they die or not: it is the spirit of adventure in the human heart. Read Mr. Roosevelt's volumes on the taming of the mighty West, read any of the myriad books about the discoverers and explorers and colonizers of new lands, and you will find their lesson just exactly that which, for one thing, is taught by the fierce rivalries of our athletic youth; namely, that man is not the namby-pamby creature that he seems to be to our more casual observation; that to baby himself and spare himself, coddle and fend himself, are not the most characteristic features of his mind. Of how many might it have been written, as it is written in the great anonymous Epistle to the Hebrews, "If they had been mindful of that country from which they set out, they had opportunity to return." Look at the Mayflower's company: half of them dead, and buried on the bleak hillside before the vessel went back in the spring; and the others, "they had opportunity to return." How many availed themselves of it? Not one. Whence came such stuff as that? All from the desire to worship God according to the dictates of their own consciences? Oh, no; not all. Some of it from the fascination of the dangers and anxieties of the new life there 'twixt the Indian devil and the deep Atlantic sea. We read in many books of the hardships which early settlers have endured, and we wonder what could tempt men to endure such things. What tempted them was the hardships, the stand-up fight with cruel oppositions, the exhilaration, the delight, the rapture of treating such things with contempt or crushing them into an inarticulate pulp under their steadily advancing feet.

Now let the young man act upon this hint as he stands upon "the threshold of life's awful temple" with "uncovered head and breathless listening," or likelier with the *nil admirari* simper on his face we know, alas! so well. Let him ask himself who are the men who are having a good time, who are glad to be alive, who are thanking God that their lives have fallen to them in such pleasant places, who would not have been born a day earlier or a day later because

"now is the accepted time and now is the day of salvation."
Who are these men? Are they the men who are dealing
softly with themselves, who are prone to cushioned ease,
who avoid everything hard and disagreeable? Are they not
rather the men who "scorn delights and live laborious
days," who, when there is hard work to be done, abuse and
contumely to be borne, gravitate to such opportunities as do
the planets to the stars about which they swing forever as
with solemn joy? It is no vain imagination, I am sure, that
a general of division can get ten men for dangerous service
— a forlorn hope it may be — easier than one to do some easy
thing; that men will tread upon each other for precedence
when wounds and death are offered, as they would not were
the call merely one for foragers where foraging would be
comfortable and safe. And I do not see why the same spirit
and the same principles should not prevail throughout the
whole of life; why men should not be fascinated and
allured by opportunities to do difficult things in other
spheres of thought and action, as well as on the play-ground
or the field of battle, as well as in the exploration of new continents and the colonization of their lonely wildernesses and
their dangerous frontiers.

We hear, and not infrequently, that we are living in degenerate times and that good courage is but little in demand,
has but few opportunities to express itself in thought or
action. And here is the very reason, some would say, why,
if there are no good wars to go to, we must have our athletics
and have them of the most strenuous and exacting kind,
making some sharp and terrible demand on a man's fearless-
ness and scorn of death. But I believe, I cannot but believe, that in our modern life as it is organized in these years
of grace, there are just as good opportunities for courage as
there ever were at any time in the world's history; just as
good as any that were offered by Grant and Sherman to
their bravest men; just as good — see how I cap the climax
— as any captain of an athletic crew has ever offered, or ever
can offer, to his men, whose muscles are like braided steel
and whose bosoms are incapable of fear.

I am speaking more particularly of the opportunities for good courage that inhere in modern life upon its higher table-lands, in its more cultivated fields; but I commend you to a recent article by President Eliot in the *Atlantic Monthly*, in which he essays to show how much of danger, and, consequently, of possible courage, are implicated in the most serviceable occupations of our ordinary life. "Think," he says, "of the locomotive engineer, the electrical lineman, the railroad brakeman, the city fireman, the police in our great cities." That he does not draw too much on his imagination is evident from the fact that in 1893 and 1894 there were 59,000 trainmen and other railroad employees killed or wounded in the United States. The trained nurse "simply in the way of duty, without the stimulus of excitement or companionship, runs risks from which many a soldier in hot blood would shrink." How true it is that "no one need be anxious about the lack of opportunities in civilized life for the display of heroic qualities." How true it is that no day of the year lacks exhibitions of a courage stout as that which drives the flying wedge into the opposing mass in glorious play or gathers quietly a sheaf of bayonets into the soldier's breast, tender with thoughts of dear ones he shall see no more! One of the finest types of this every-day courage goes by the vilest name. The man possessing it is called a "scab." "In defence of his rights as an individual he deliberately incurs the reprobation of many of his fellows, and runs the immediate risk of bodily injury and even death." This is but one of many illustrations that President Eliot has brought forward to support his thesis that our industrial civilization has opportunities for courage equal to the most warlike periods of the past. He has other illustrations which bring the matter home to the most cultivated men, and show how little ground they have for fear that, when their foot-ball days are over, all their heroic occupations will be gone, unless somebody at Washington succeeds in trumping up a war with England or some less formidable antagonist. One of these illustrations is so fine,

so apt, and so impressive, that I cannot deny myself the
pleasure of giving you the whole passage, a thing I seldom
do,— lest a mere reference to it should leave you ignorant of
its force. "Another modern personage," he says, "who
needs heroic endurance, and often exhibits it, is the public
servant who steadily does his duty against the outcry of a
party press bent on perverting his every word and act.
Through the telegram, cheap postage, and the daily newspaper, the forces of hasty public opinion can now be concen-
trated and expressed with a rapidity and intensity unknown
to preceding generations. In consequence, the independent
thinker or actor or the public servant, when his thoughts or
acts run counter to prevailing popular or party opinions,
encounters sudden and intense obloquy, which, to many
temperaments, is very formidable. That habit of submitting
to the opinion of the majority, which democracy fosters,
renders the storm of detraction and calumny all the more
difficult to endure,— makes it, indeed, so intolerable to many
citizens that they will conceal or modify their opinions
rather than endure it. . . . This habit of partisan ridicule
and denunciation in the daily reading-matter for millions of
people calls for a new kind of courage and toughness in
public men, not in brief moments of excitement only, but
steadily, year in and year out." That President Eliot was
not drawing on his imagination here I was convinced anew
when almost simultaneously with the appearance of his
article I read of the re-election of a man to Congress who
had amply shown this sort of courage. You may think his
re-election is convincing, that his case was not so serious after
all. But he could not see that re-election through the blinding hail of partisan detraction and abuse a year or two ago.
What he thought he saw was the complete collapse and ruin
of his political aspirations ; and yet he went right on. Give
our political societies time enough, and they generally come
to their senses and applaud the men they cursed most heartily.

"Far in front the cross stands ready, and the crackling fagots burn,
While the hooting mob of yesterday with silent awe return
To glean up the scattered ashes into history's golden urn,"

or to re-elect the honest congressmen; but neither of these possible events does much to brace the courage of the man who stands four-square to all the winds that blow, as from the mouth of hell.

Here is a particular instance taken from our political conditions, but the opportunities they furnish for good courage are not few and far between. The corruption of our political system means the opportunity for highest courage in our men of light and leading. "The brave man's hope is the coward's excuse." The coward's excuse for letting politics alone is that they are so miserably corrupt. The brave man's hope is that he can do something to better them. And, setting out to do so, the endeavor has not been all trouble and anxiety by a good deal. As in Sarah Battle's whist, there has been "the rigor of the game" and the corresponding satisfaction and elation. Theodore Roosevelt and Colonel Waring have not had a bed of roses to lie on; but, like the Indian yogi, they have rather come to like their bed of spikes. How much of base concession and of its political remuneration do you imagine it would have taken to give Governor Greenhalge of Massachusetts a tithe of the divine exhilaration that he got from braving once, twice, and again the rage of partisans who thought, and seemed entirely justified in thinking, that they held his political future in the hollow of their itching palms? When our Brooke Herford mourned to Phillips Brooks what long, slow, uphill work it was getting the good cause fairly started on its triumphant way, the great preacher answered, "Yes, but what fun it is!" What fun it always is to fight a good fight, to keep the faith, to stand up and be shot at for the dear love of some great principle, or concrete social or political advantage! Why, there are thousands of young men in our great cities, graduates of our colleges and universities, wondering why nothing seems to stir their pulses now as did the dear old athletic games,— and all the time the air they breathe is that of an Augean stable, which, if they should go in to clean it, would give them such a tussle as they never had behind the flying ball, and such fun, too, as they never had in driving it beyond the line of victory.

But I must not draw my illustrations too exclusively from the political field. Every young man should be a politician in some sort. He should be interested in politics; he should understand them, not merely as they are rendered in the high lights of a political canvass, but as they are rendered on the historian's juster page. But for most men politics must be an organ of self-sacrificing devotion to the common weal. They must look elsewhere for a livelihood. And there are those who tell us that it is impossible for any one to amass a fortune within the limits of our industrial system, and be at the same time an honest man. I do not believe it. I should be most miserably unhappy if I did. But then, if *you* think so, or *you*, or *you*, there is your work cut out; there is your opportunity for heroic action plain enough,— to go without the fortune that cannot be honestly amassed. The thing that most impresses me is this: to what a vast extent, for all our checks and balances, the stability of the business community depends upon "the unbought grace of life," the spontaneous honesty of innumerable men. But there can, I think, be no doubt that, with the increasing intricacy and complexity of our modern business organization, the temptations to wrong doing are much greater than they were formerly. The prizes contended for are much greater. The avoidance of personal responsibility appears to be much less difficult. Now let the man who mourns the loss of such great opportunities for personal courage as the military age could boast, and who thinks that our athletics cannot be too brutal if haply they may furnish something of the chance to be heroic and enduring that the men of old enjoyed,— let such a man be set well in the midst of our great business field, its splendid prizes shining in his eyes, opportunities offering continually to make ten dollars instead of one dollar by doing something just a little bit "irregular," or winking at another man's irregularity, and if he does not have all the opportunities for the exercise of a manly courage that he wants

he must have a stomach for such things of Falstaffian proportions. The temptations which beset the business man are
many. One of the most common is to depreciate the value
of his goods, once he has got his market, and so double his
profits for a few years before he is found out. But this is
one of the most gross, and the man who succumbs to it must
be pretty nearly dead already in trespasses and sins. There
are others which are very subtle in their operation. Subtle
or gross, their name is legion ; and the man of business who
is to meet them and to conquer them has no holiday affair
upon his hands. The decision may mean poverty instead
of riches, or, at the best, the merest competency instead of
"growing rich beyond the dreams of avarice." Let him that
thinketh he standeth take heed lest he fall. Let him who
thinks there is no opportunity for courage in the sphere of
business keep well the law of perfect honesty and truth in
all his dealings for one uneventful day.

New types of courage are developed by new conditions in
the political and industrial and religious world. The ethics
of theological transition furnish one of the most conspicuous
of these in our own time. Nothing is more popular and
attractive in our time than the preaching of heretical
doctrines in orthodox pulpits, the preacher generally finding
some ingenious excuse for damning those who have said his
good things before him. Nothing is more popular and
attractive than this sort of thing, but nothing is more dangerous. There came to me last Sunday evening, after Dr.
Savage's installation, an Episcopal clergyman, who said : " I
am as good a Unitarian as you. But I asked President
Eliot," he continued, "how his university methods would do
for little children. Little children must have their kin-
dergarten, and, as an Episcopalian clergyman, I am a religious kindergartner." And he seemed to think I would
applaud him for thus making himself accursed for his brethren's sake. But I could not find it in my heart to do so.
What I said was, that the religious kindergartner should
believe in his own toys. But what I wished to say was

something you know pretty well, the great adjuration of Carlyle,—"Go to perdition if thou must, but with a lie in thy mouth? by the Eternal Maker, no!"

Moral athletics here in great abundance; chances for the exercises of good courage not a few. The story of "Robert Elsmere" was written that the thoughts of many hearts might be revealed. To-day there are hundreds, if not thousands, of ministers, standing in orthodox pulpits, who do not believe the traditional orthodoxy any more than you or I. What shall they do? They can stay where they are, and preach what they like, so long as they do not say, "This is the thing called heresy, and it *is* what it is *called*." But it takes courage, a great deal of courage, to do that. On the one hand is comfort, ease, applause; on the other, nobody · knows what. Heresy in orthodox pulpits is the taking and the paying thing. Heresy in heretical pulpits is quite another matter. And do not imagine for a moment that all the "good courages" in the religious sphere are reserved for the heretical preachers. The most orthodox have their opportunities of standing on the weaker side against the vested wrong; and laymen, young and old, can follow their convictions into the unpopular church, and work for it, and make sacrifices for it, or "bow down in the house of Rimmon",— go with the multitude that keep holy day, having an eye to windward, whence may blow to them some social or personal advantage, some business connection, or some eligible match.

There is an aspect of this matter of moral athletics, athletic morals, which is more strictly personal. Men, young and old, have their besetting sins. I need not specify. You know the motley crew. Now if a man really wants a good fight, a good opportunity for courage and endurance, let him stand up to one of these and fight with it till he is standing with his heel upon its head. And the parable is not for men alone. The athletic figure of speech may not be well adapted to the feminine gender. But women, too, have their besetting sins, and no metaphor is needed to exaggerate their ugly force, nor can exaggerate the courage which it takes for them to overcome them and from the sordid conflict rise into that height of glorified and perfect womanhood which is the brightest boon that heaven has for earth.

In these personal conflicts one of the hard conditions is that they have no spectators to applaud the things well done, to nerve the wavering strength. My friend is thoroughly convinced that he or I could furnish all the courage needed for such a game as that which Princeton won the other day if we had twenty thousand people shouting like devils in our ears. He might, but as for me,— well, I would rather not be tried. But that the twenty thousand shouters make all courage easier there cannot be a particle of doubt. It is of the very essence of the situation that in so many of our personal conflicts with temptation we have to stand up to our work alone. Alone, yet not alone ; else was Apollos, or whoever wrote the great Epistle to the Hebrews, much mistaken when he said, " Therefore, seeing that we are compassed about by so great a cloud of witnesses, let us lay aside every weight, and the sin which doth so easily beset us, and let us run with patience the race set before us." And in these struggles of the inner life, these battles with inveterate faults, with selfish dispositions, with impure desires, is it not as if we were Childe Roland in the desperate pass, and all around us were the friends, alive and dead, who have always expected us to do well and to whom we have given bonds of memory and hope and secret tears never to disappoint their gracious trust ? Seeing that we are compassed about by *such* a cloud of witnesses, how dare we play our parts unworthily ?

> " Here eyes do regard you
> In Eternity's stillness ;
> Here is all fulness
> Ye brave to reward you ;
> Work and despair not."

A LIBERAL FAITH.

SAID Phillips Brooks in one of his discourses, "We talk a great deal in these days about a liberal faith. What is a liberal faith, my friends? It seems to me that by every true meaning of the word, by every true thought of the idea, a liberal faith in one that believes much, and not a faith that believes little." With this expression of the great preacher's personal conviction I find myself heartily agreed; and what I wish to do this morning is to expand his thought, to distinguish a faith that believes much from one that believes little, and to distinguish certain forms of thought and feeling that are considered liberal from certain others that have a better right to be considered so. But if a liberal faith is the faith that believes much and not little, who are there that believe so much as the most credulous people? I know that many will say this, and I am the more glad on this account that I find Phillips Brooks declaring, " It is true, indeed, that, as soon as a man becomes eager for belief, for the truth of God, and for the mysteries with which God's universe is filled, he becomes all the more critical and careful. He will no longer, if he were before, be simply greedy of things to believe, so that if any superstition comes offering itself to him, he will gather it in indiscriminately and believe it without evidence, without examination. He becomes all the more critical and careful the more he becomes assured that belief and not unbelief is the true condition of his life." Here I must bid Phillips Brooks good-by and go the remainder of my way alone. The truth would seem to be, that, in the best possible meaning of the term, a liberal faith is not a liberal disposition in the matter of belief; that is, a disposition to believe much, and especially much of that which has been traditionally handed down. It is a faith whose contents are liberal, whose thoughts of God and man and life and destiny are broad and deep and high.

Notice, in this connection, that here, as in the art of reading books, *non multa, sed multum* is the rule,— not many things, but much. There are men, for instance, who believe a hundred things about God and those who believe thirty-three or thirty-nine (so many and no more) who do not believe *in* him so much as some others whose articles of belief are only two or three. The quality of the belief is much. And this also is to be remembered : that the credulous, the greedy mind is not confined to those who are most open-mouthed to swallow the traditional belief. The passing time is very much like that which corresponded to the first centuries of Christianity and the last centuries of the Roman paganism. As we look back upon that time, we see that the most credu-lous people were not those who clung to the old faith and ordinance : they were those who abandoned themselves to one or another of the many forms of new belief which, simul-taneously with Christianity, were pressing on the Roman mind. And in our own time the most credulous are certainly not always those who swallow the traditional doctrines of religion as readily as if these were strawberries and cream : they are those — their name is legion — who are so hungry for the things which they have needlessly foregone that they snatch at anything which comes to them noisily advertised as the bread which cometh down from heaven. They are those who have gone the whole length of negation, only to tumble over finally into an abyss of bottomless credulity. Even among those who have not tumbled over, but are very near the edge, you will often find a more absolute credulity than in the traditionalists to whom they are most violently op-posed. We are obliged, sometimes, to entertain a doubt whether this boasted age of science will not, from the stand-point of the future, seem pre-eminently superstitious.

A liberal faith is neither the credulity of the traditionalist nor the credulity of crude, irrational negation and mere cob-

web speculation. And no more is it that slackness of indifference which so frequently imagines itself worthy of the
name, and representative of the thing. Of this slackness of
indifference we have a great abundance in our time. It has
domesticated itself in the conventional churches. The
young person seeking admission to their communion is assured that it really makes very little difference what he
believes. There are the creeds and articles, to be sure, but
they are historical documents : they are preserved to indicate
what was formerly believed, and they are subscribed to or
recited with the tacit or explicit understanding that they are
subject to individual diminution or addition or interpretation. This slackness of indifference is the veriest Proteus
and has many forms. One is the ecclesiastical, which I have
already named. Another is the scientific, which resolves religion into a mere sentiment, declaring that it has no intellectual contents; and there are found students and teachers
of religion who have sunk so low that they meekly and thank-
fully accept the crust that is thus thrown to them by those
who sit at groaning tables in the great hall of science. The
philosophical form of this Proteus is much the same. Its
doctrine is, that just as we may digest our food and live a
healthy life without any knowledge of physiology, so we may
digest our sentiments and duties and live a healthy, moral,
and religious life without ethical or theological reflection.
The antithesis of reason and faith is not more definite with
those who, in the traditional manner, regard faith as a sup-
plementary faculty whereby men can attain truth without
reason, or in spite of reason, than it often is with our philosophers ; nor more contemptuous of reason than are these.
They present this funny paradox : by the use of reason they
would convince us that reason is of no account.

The slackness of indifference takes on another and more
popular form. "What difference does it make," we hear,
"what a man believes? Theology is not religion." And
the corollary of this proposition is sometimes one thing and
sometimes another,—sometimes abstention from all public

recognition of religion, but oftener adhesion to the particular church which is most convenient or most fashionable or most socially engaging, though it may be the most orthodox in the community. The churches of the traditional theology are largely re-enforced by men and women who are aiding and abetting what they cannot possibly believe, and encouraging the preacher in a course destructive of his moral character and his self-respect. If sometimes more consistent and con-scientious people protest with these for countenancing and supporting things which they do not believe, the answer is that they believe them as much as anybody. It is not true, and it would not absolve them if it were. Two wrongs, or two hundred, cannot make a right.

Religion is degraded when it is made a mush of sentiment, and denied all intellectual significance. Theology, that once queened it over all the arts and science, does not propose to abdicate her throne. Here is a science that can hold up its head among the best. Some one has said that metaphysics is the finding of bad reasons for what we know by instinct, but it is an instinct to seek those reasons. Good! and if theology is the finding of reasons bad or good for many things that are spontaneous in our spiritual nature, the find-ing of these reasons is as spontaneous for humanity in gen-eral as for men to breathe or sleep. Nor do I know anything more honorable to humanity than the finding of the same reasons, the seeking of them if they have not and cannot be truly found. It would be a miserable race of men that could live in such a world as this and not try to fathom its mystery, not try to name aright the power that surges through it in a tide whose waves are ages of immeasurable time. Over and over again, now by the philosopher and anon by the scientist, we are reminded of the limits of religious thought, and of the presumption of endeavoring to tear away the veil of the Un-knowable. But the only way of finding out what is unknow-able is by pushing ever forward the limits of the known. For Socrates, the presumptuous thing was to seek to pene-trate that region which is now commensurate with the whole

field of natural science. Think of the loss if men had been
obedient to his word! Yet was he a very great philosopher.
Wherefore, even though some very great philosophers of our
own time would interdict us from that sphere of the divine
activity which theology endeavors to explore, let us go on re-
gardless of their prohibition. Seeing that we cannot know
anything without knowing something of Him who is all in all,
the very science that arrays itself against theology is nothing
if not theological. The Unknown is a mighty sea that
surges round about the known with ceaseless ebb and flow.
How much of it is unknowable mankind will know a great
deal better fifty or a hundred thousand years hence than it
does now. In the mean time the presumption is in fixing
any limit to the intellectual force which already has achieved
so much.

Do we not congratulate ourselves unduly on a state of
things whose characteristic note is the inability to distinguish
things that differ, an easy-going assurance that one system of
theology is about as good as another? This sort of thing is
what a great many people mean by liberality. But where
does the liberality come in if there is no particular difference? A man without much effort or without doing himself
any particular credit may be liberal enough to tolerate his
natural face in a glass, or his theological opinions reflected
in another man's. But what we want is the liberality that can
be tolerant of the most radical difference from one's own
opinions. There was better stuff for making manly men in
the old dogmatism and bigotry than in the liberality which
can tolerate every possible difference of opinion because it
has not a conviction of its own. We have had our World's
Parliament of Religions, and very beautiful it was in many
ways. It brought out the unity in diversity, but it also
brought out the diversity in unity, and I am not sure
that this was not the more important lesson. There are
those who have a vision of the different religions, stripped
every one of its peculiar qualities, and of a world-wide unity
of religion compounded of the simple common elements that

would remain. It will come, perhaps, when men and women wear only the most necessary clothing and eat only the most necessary food. Let us hope it will not come before. For how much better than any uniformity like that of the primeval fiery cloud is a diversity like that of the firmament we know, thick set with stars, one star differing from another star in glory, the different religions clothing the nakedness of their common substance of belief with the many colored draperies of their several and diverse historical traditions! And how much better in each particular community the clear-cut conviction, and the manly difference of manly men, than the good-natured indifference of sheer mental laziness, or the unqualified homogeneity that would invite no splendid rivalries of athletic minds, no generous mutual toleration on the part of men whose doctrines are as inconvertible as ice and fire !

True liberality is every way desirable, and it never shows more beautiful than when associated with a theology that is severe and hard. As between such liberality and liberal opinion, as we designate opinion that is free from the bondage of traditional authority, there is no question which has the greater *moral* beauty. The liberal opinion, as such, may not have any : it may have come to a man as naturally as the air he breathes ; or it may be the result of a moral heroism that can hardly be surpassed. We have no more burnings for heresy, and you may think we have no more persecution : but here in Brooklyn there are men and women suffering for their liberal opinion's sake pangs not less horrible than those of wheel and stake. Those were self-limiting : they made an end of both the sufferer and suffering; but these go on year after year,— the averted looks, the bitter accusations, the old-time sympathy and affection cruelly withheld. I speak of what I know and testify to that which I have seen. But even here the moral beauty is not in the liberal belief, but in the openness of mind and the indomitable will to seek the truth, let who will favor or forbear. Happy are they who have both liberal opinion and that liberality which can be patient with the utmost difference! They do not always go together. There is a radical bigotry as intolerant as that of the most intolerant conservatism of our time. If one must be denied us or the other, let it by all means be the liberal opinion. Better the theology of Calvin with the liberality of Channing than the theology of Channing with the bigotry of Calvin : difficult and rare associations both, but not impossible. Reading the Life of Dean Stanley, some of us have been disappointed in his opinions,— that they were not more liberal. But we have been more than compensated by his liberality,— his genial tolerance of beliefs that differed from his own through a wide range of difference and opposition. There was nothing mean or stinted about that. And it was all the more beautiful because it was not the expression of any intellectual indifference, and because his toleration was for those on either side of him, the more radical and the less. Some "good Unitarians," who are none too good, might profitably consider his example. For some of them can be very sweet and pleasant to the difference on one side of their own opinion, but cannot be anything but intolerant of the side which is away from their own tendency, whatever that may be.

True liberality is every way desirable, and so is liberal opinion ; but neither true liberality nor liberal opinion answers to the full-orbed significance of a liberal faith. Either of these is better than mere open-mouthed credulity, whether directed to the oldest or the newest things, or mere slack indifference. But there are men whose liberality is beautiful who have but little faith. There are pessimists who have none at all, who are nothing if not tolerant of the most diverse opinions,— for them so many diverse symptoms of that intolerable disease which we call life. And to be convinced that liberal opinion does not necessarily imply a liberal faith, we need only take some representative of liberal opinion in whom the freedom from traditional limitations is only equalled by the lack of faith in man or God. Such an one was Professor Huxley. Surely, no one of his contemporaries was more free than he in his opinions, less able or anxious to conform them to traditional lines. But had he a liberal faith? Does it look so when he says, "Even the best of modern civilizations appears to me to exhibit a condition of mankind which neither embodies any worthy ideal nor even possesses the merit of stability"? Does it look so when he continues, "I do not hesitate to express the opinion that, if there is no hope of a large improvement of the condition of the greater part of the human family, if it is true that the increase of knowledge, the winning of a greater dominion over nature which is its consequence, and the wealth which follows upon that dominion, are to make no difference in the extent and the intensity of want, with its concomitant physical and moral degradation among the masses of the people, I should hail the advent of some kindly comet, which would sweep the whole affair away, as a desirable consummation"?

Even here we have a certain faith, no doubt,— a faith in the ideal and a faith in the ability of men, in spite of Nature's enmity, to make the good things better and the bad things good. But surely it is not a liberal faith which holds that what men do achieve must be achieved in spite of Nature's enmity; nor is it a liberal faith which holds that, in some half a million years of various experiments, men have achieved so little that the hope of the race is in its extinction unless it can do much better. A liberal faith does not so read the creed of evolution as to hold that all the generations of the past have been merely so many rounds by which the coming man has climbed to that on which he now stands, far, far below the top. It holds that every generation, every stage of the advance, has been a good thing in itself, if not the best thing possible. Mivart, a pious Roman Catholic, has so far disengaged himself from the cosmology of Genesis that he accepts Sir William Thomson's estimate of the period during which life has existed on our planet — one hundred million years! So, then, for ninety-nine and a half millions the creatures were waiting for the manifestation of the sons of God. But they did not know that they were waiting; and they had a good time all the while, after a fashion of their own. And it is to repeat the folly and the egotism of the old theology,— questioning "Doth God care for oxen?" and answering, "Certainly not, these things are for our sakes,"— to imagine that those ninety-nine million, five hundred thousand years of animal life had no justification save as their dust became the soil from which the human race should spring. Be ours the liberal faith that, if the crowning race had never come, Wisdom would have been justified of her children in the mud and scum of things: Be ours the liberal faith that all the generations of mankind have had their justification in their immediate satisfactions. struggles, victories, whatever further justification they may have had in their reaching forward to the crowning age of ages, where,

"On the glimmering summits far withdrawn,
God makes himself an awful rose of dawn."

A liberal faith — I come back to my original definition — is a faith the contents of which are liberal, whose quality is confident and brave, whose thoughts of God and man and destiny are broad and deep and high. Ye believe in God. says a New Testament Epistle; ye do well: the devils also believe, and tremble. Now the faith that has the quality of such belief is not a liberal faith, however perfectly assured. The habitual action of a liberal faith is not to make a man tremble, but to steady him and stiffen him, to brace him for the adverse shocks of circumstance. Seeing that God is infinite, it would seem that any true faith in him must be a liberal faith. And, indeed, it is so. But we must not be fooled with words. We can believe in a man's existence and yet have no faith in him, and it is exactly so with God. When we believe in a man, as we say, then we have faith in him. We have a sweet and joyous confidence in his integrity and justice and humanity that is not shaken by this or that isolated circumstance which we cannot at once adjust to it. So with our faith in God. What we believe *about* him does not so much matter,—not so much, and yet we must not be disdainful here, for what we believe about him has a very potent influence in its mass and aggregation on our belief *in* him. But our belief *in* him is the thing that counts.

And whence comes this belief? Not wholly from the sweep of science gathering in the facts of cosmic order to build up its splendid generalizations. If it were not so, it would go hard with the majority of men and women whose scientific knowledge is no great affair. Yet these also have their life to live. If they could live in the moment only, if they might never stop and think, it might be well enough till sickness came, or ruinous misfortune, or the death of precious friends. But they cannot live in the moment; they must sometimes stop to think; if their own affairs do not oblige them to, then others' pain and sorrow press on their hearts. Moreover, if they go to the scientific people for the faith they need, they are sometimes sent away uncomforted. There are men very wise in science who have very little faith in God. That is because of their intense engrossment with some particular part which makes the broader look impossible. They save others; themselves they cannot save. The chastisement of our peace is upon them, and by their stripes we are healed. What then? Shall we fall back on the old antithesis of faith and science? God forbid! Far from us be any such book-keeping by double entry! But our science must look in, as well as out. The facts of the inner life are no less substantial than the facts of the astronomer and the geologist. And these facts are as "all compact" of faith in God as the stars are of atoms, as the interstellar spaces are of the ether which eye hath not seen but science has conceived.

"The stream cannot rise higher than the fountain": that is good science. "Nothing is evolved which is not first involved": so is that. "Can mortal man be more just than God?" that also; and "God is greater than our hearts." The attraction of gravitation and the law of the radius vector are not more sure than are these laws of man's reflection of the life of God.   They mean that we cannot conceive or hope or dream of anything better than the divine reality.   We may not accept the Fourth Gospel as a valid testimony to the life and words of Jesus.   We cannot do so.   And therefore we cannot believe he ever said, when Philip wished to see the Father, " He that hath seen me hath seen the Father."   But he might have said as much, and so might thousands of others, men and women.   Might, but *could* not ; for those who do most to reveal the Father are ever slowest to lay claim to such a revelation.   All human goodness is a revelation of God's goodness, but the highest revelation is the voice of one's own heart.   We have known men and women so full of loving help and tenderness, so full of sweet encouragement and divine compassion, that we have said, " A God as good as these is good enough for me ! " and at the same time we have known that his goodness is inclusive of ten thousand times ten thousand such examples, and, beyond that, incalculably more and more.   It is only the merest tyro who imagines that our scientific knowledge is limited to the visible world.   Tyndall indoctrinated us in the scientific uses of the imagination, and showed us that there was an ideal extension of our knowledge infinite in scope beyond the visible.   There is no sounder science than the ideal extension through all the infinity of God of the goodness which is known to us.   Happy are we if we know many bright examples of the goodness which invites to such ideal extension ; but happier if we also have in our own hearts the goodness which is prophecy and pledge of the eternal and divine.

> " Do I find love so full in my nature, God's ultimate gift,
> And doubt his own love can compete with it,— here the parts shift,
> Here the creature surpass the creator, the end what began ? "

To do that — so to find and so to doubt — were as illogical, as unphilosophical, as unscientific, as absurd, as to find two things equal to the same thing and yet doubt that they are equal to each other.

It follows from this vital dependence of our faith in God upon our faith in man that we cannot have a liberal faith in God without a liberal faith in man. And such a faith is quite inseparable from any large appreciation of the course of human history,— the arts men have developed, the tasks they have accomplished, the civilizations they have reared, the inventions and discoveries by which they have subdued the original harshness of the earth, the sciences that have revealed the boundless mystery and order of the world, the heroisms that have sustained good causes and made bad causes almost good by the splendor of their absolute devotion. Nor less this faith sustains itself by visions of the possibilities of human nature projected for us by the exceptional splendor of great deeds which have lit up the centuries, and by such brave fidelities as we ourselves have known, of one substance with the fidelity of Jesus and all great and holy souls, as good as any ever shown by martyrs at the stake, which flame could not destroy or make one fraction less. Why, friends, if the Almighty were not good, but evil utterly, I think that he would soon or late be shamed into all sweet benevolence by the spectacle of human excellence, the golden deeds that men and women have so bravely and so sweetly done. That is a very lovely story which Dr. Abbott tells us about the young girl who came to him wishing to join the church, and he asked her, "Do you wish to be like Christ?" and she answered, "I wish to be like my mother." Oh, happy mother, to deserve that perfect praise! Oh, happy world, in which it is deserved by tens of thousands of each generation! And when Jesus loved to say "Our Father!" how near was Nazareth to Brooklyn, his thought to that of the dear girl who answered Dr. Abbott in that blessed way! And how tenderly Theodore Parker took up her thought and that of Jesus and blended them in sweet accord in his habitual prayer, "O Thou who art our Father and our Mother": Thus evermore inextricable is our liberal faith in man and God.

I have shown how far removed from liberal faith in God

may be mere liberal opinion. It may be as far removed from liberal faith in man. In fact, we must go to Calvin for any estimate of human nature so contemptuous and so contemptible as that of certain modern thinkers and reformers, who arrogate to themselves the sole representation of liberal opinion, and who think they have a faith in man so liberal that there is no other that is worthy to be called liberal in comparison. For it is utterly illogical to believe in man as he now is, or as some few hundreds of particular men are, while holding that all the generations of the past and all the present race, some few thousands excepted, have been and are insane and idiotic in their religious mind. Yet that they have been and are insane and idiotic is undeniable if there has been no reality in the religious hopes, beliefs, and aspirations of the past. The hope of the race would be in its extinction if these things were true, and Huxley's comet could not come too soon. But those who have a liberal faith in human nature will not accept as true the railing accusation that has been brought against it by some thinkers of our time, who do not think too much. They will believe that there has always been a reality in religion, however irrational its manifestation. They will believe,

> "That the feeble hands and helpless,
> Groping blindly in the darkness,
> Touch God's right hand in that darkness,"

and by that touch are thrilled with something better than the haughty sciolism of the half-educated intellect, which makes its ignorance the test of others' knowledge, and its self-sufficiency the condemnation of the multitude who, in all ages, have said with the apostle, "Our sufficiency is of God."

The same apostle said, "I have fought a good fight; I have kept the faith." Now, in this busy, work-day world of ours, we are so circumstanced that we have not only our own faith to keep but that of other men. Doubtless men are not so scientific as they should be in their reasoning from day to day. Doubtless if they understood the logic of induction better they would not argue from the turpitude of one man or woman, or even a dozen or twenty, to the essential turpitude of human nature and the injustice or indifference of the Almighty. But nothing is surer than that they do argue in this way continually, and that any base or even thoughtless man or woman can do more to destroy the faith of others in a day than Paley's "Natural Theology," or even the best things of Martineau, could do to rebuild it in a year. And, therefore, it is not enough that we shall carefully consider what we can do to make our own faith in God and man more liberal, and sweet, and glad. We must consider also what we can do to make the faith of others after the pattern we ourselves have seen in mounts of vision, haunts of silent prayer; what we must *not* do, that would, if done, hasten the swift inference from our baseness to the baseness of mankind and to the divine indifference to human good or ill. Happy are they whose goodness daily builds anew, in human hearts, faith in humanity and God! — thrice happy, seeing that it is a divine impossibility that they should do this service to their fellow-men, and not at the same time build up, in ever stronger and more glorious fashion, their own sweet and blessed confidence in all mankind and in him who is over all, God blessed forever.

THE CONTINUING CITY.*

THE complaint of the New Testament writer that he and
his fellow Christians had no continuing city is one that
sometimes finds a very literal echo in the modern heart.
Schiller's notable saying, There is nothing changeless but
change, is nowhere found more true than in the cities of
to-day,—miracles of impermanence, the waster and the
builder too forever at their work, the march of improvement signalized by perpetual sapping and mining, with up-
heaval as by earthquake shocks. The cities of Europe are
much stabler than our own; but in the most venerable of
them all — Rome, the Eternal City of the poet and the rheto-
rician — we found a lively transformation scene was being
everywhere displayed. The Appian Way was choked with
carts loaded with materials for new buildings destined to
replace the old ; and when we went to the Fountain of Trevi,
and threw in our *soldi* and drank the water for augury of
our return some happy day, they told us that we must not
long delay or there would be no Fountain of Trevi pouring
its flood of diamonds into the emerald pool below, that
some smart new street was going to obliterate it from men's
sight forever. I think it has not done so yet.

But of course the New Testament writer was not troub-
ling his spirit over such little things as these. Little he
cared for the impermanence of Jerusalem or Ephesus or
Antioch or Rome. He looked for a city that had foundations, whose builder and maker was God ; a Jerusalem the
golden, like that of the Apocalyptic vision coming down from
God out of heaven prepared as a bride adorned for her
husband. And so it happens that his meaning was not one

* Preached on the first Sunday of the year.

that comes home to us more forcibly or appealingly than our trivial application of his words would have come home to him. Whatever hopes we cherish of new life, new love, new opportunity, upon the other side of death, they reflect no discredit on the world that now is. We shall be satisfied if we find anything there so beautiful and good as the things which here delight us and sustain us, sense and soul. We remember Dr. Holmes's poem, "Homesick in Heaven," and we wonder if we shall not sometimes be homesick for the dear old mountains of the earth and the multitudinous laughter of the sea; yes, and for the faces and the voices that we knew of old, if they are different there. If different, they cannot be so good, whatever angel-folk may think or say.

> " Hours fugitive as precious return! return!
> Let the old life once more enmesh us!"

Moreover, we have *here* a continuing city. So had the New Testament writer, only it did not exist for his imagination; and what does not exist for the imagination does not practically exist at all. It is the City of Dateless Time. How long has been, how long will be, its secret and sublime continuance? Once it began for men as yesterday, and to-morrow it would cease to be. Now the six thousand years of Bible reckoning are not a drop in the bucket to the millions that have come and gone since first the starry tides set toward the centre of the fluid haze and eddied into suns that wheeling cast the planets. And in "the nature of the times deceased," as Shakspere said, "there is a history, the which observed, a man may prophesy with a near aim of the main chance of things as yet not come to life," and know that they will have as free a scope, as boundless a duration, as the things already gone. And in this vast continuance there is no break.

The days and years are correspondent with the earth's revolution on its axis and around the sun; and these obvious motions serve our convenience excellently well, yet have in them as little of the essential quality of time as has a yardstick of the stuff it measures off. The new year did not always begin with January, and the old reckoning had the virtue of a nearer correspondence with the year's solar history. And so it happens that all the emotions which now seem so proper to this parting of the ways — the backward and the forward look, the regrets for wrong things done and things undone that should have been performed, the resolutions and the hopes with which the future beckons and exhilarates our hearts — are only artificially related to the passing time. If the old reckoning had been kept they would have clung to that with the same energy with which they now cling to the new ; and if a new reckoning should be adopted, making any other day of all the year the first, all of our new-year emotions would betake themselves to that, like migratory birds, and all the old-year emotions to the immediately preceding days. Do not imagine, therefore, that you can choose your own old year and new, and transfer to them all of the old-year and new-year emotions that now cluster round December 31 and January 1. We are the dupes of our own artifices and arrangements. Our social nature has adjusted itself to the present order. It is as real for us as if it had a rational basis, an essential quality. If by universal agreement some other day should be made the first of the new year, long afterward there would be found the old emotions springing up about the former starting-place and goal, like garden roses where there was once a house and home, or like the seaside flowers which bloom upon the shores of Lake Superior in memory of a time when the waters of the lake were salt as the Atlantic's waves.

No continuing city? We have not only the City of Dateless Time, of unbroken temporal sequence, but also the City of Organic Evolution. Many and great have been those who have labored for the building of this city in which now we dwell secure. One of the greatest of them all (I speak of Herbert Spencer) has but just now completed the great system of philosophy which he conceived thirty-six years ago, now seeing what he then foresaw.

Of this same city Darwin was a master-builder; Tyndall another; Huxley another; and Haeckel and Wallace and Gray, and a great company besides filled with their spirit, have added street to street, and tower to tower, and spire to spire, and made the walls impregnable against the assault of superstition and the traditional theology. Here is a city of God that binds together in one grand conception all that was disparate and fragmentary in the old order of belief. For innumerable special creations,—the mud-pie of the urchin working in the sedimented pool furnishing the style of the divine activity,—we have now one eternal process sweeping through all times and things; each present bound to every future and to every past by a genetic bond, each kind to every other; the production of species by natural selection and the preservation of the fittest.

> "A subtle change of countless rings
> The next unto the farthest brings;
> The eye reads omens where it goes,
> And speaks all languages the rose;
> And striving to be man, the worm
> Mounts through all the spires of form."

"That they all may be one," prays the New Testament. Jesus and our nineteenth-century science adopts that glorious prayer, making it more glorious by expanding its "all" from a little company of the great Teacher's friends to a great company, a mighty company, that includes all human and all animal races, all suns and moons and stars. What a continuing city have we here; continuous in time, continuous in the unbroken sequence of its development, continuous in the present, actual relation of each part with every other! How the conception dwarfs the former, with its mechanic deity now pottering at this and now at that, from time to time the machinery breaking down and the maker coming round to patch it up! How it rebukes the equally mechanical conception of society and politics and religion which was the current stock of radical opinion about a century ago! Concerning nothing else was Thomas Paine so eloquent as the iniquity of one generation's making laws and institutions for another. Rub it all out and begin again, was his device for general reformation. An easy thing to say; a harder one to do. The parchment proved a palimpsest and the old writing far more indestructible than the new, which had been written over it with ink of blood and tears. Like the German kobold on the household cart, some impish spirit of the past attends all new departures, stamping on them his sign and seal. And with the consciousness of this there has come into our thought of the past something very different from the old superstitious reverence for it as a good thing in itself, and as different from the old radical contempt for it as intrinsically bad,— something very tender for its faults and glad of its intense humanity, working the designing priest far less assiduously, finding in human nature a sufficient explanation of the domination of religion and of the priest himself. The general outcome has been immensely favorable to our judgment of the past. Our constructions of individual conduct here and there may be as stern as ever; but for the general aspects of the past, however harsh, however superstitious, we are developing a very tender side, considering ourselves lest we also be too sternly judged by those who, coming after us, shall find our social and political and religious methods very far from their ideal of what is right and good.

No continuing city! Nay, but this phrase for many in our time, as for the early followers of Jesus, has a much deeper sense than any so far named. For there are those who have no continuity of purpose, no persistency of will, no constancy to an ideal, to bind together youth and manhood and old age into a unity of character in which they may abide with perfect confidence and into which their friends and all the world may enter without fear of ambush or of open harm. It is the first step which costs, the proverb says, but frequently it is one long subsequent to the first which costs the most. The mountain-climber starts off at a run,— the novice not the experienced mountaineer. *He* saves his strength for the last stages of the long ascent, where the way is steep and a foothold sometimes hard to find and the strong winds buffet like a mace. Many are the proverbs that furnish to this principle, circumstance and illustration. *He that endureth to the end* shall be saved, says the New Testament, and there, too, is the parable of the virgins, with their exhausted lamps, their lack of reserve power, and that of the hungry man at midnight who would have three loaves and got them because of his persistency. Everybody knows of Robert Bruce's instruction in this virtue from the spider who after half a dozen vain attempts to stretch his web made a seventh trial with better luck. And a good many know of Mr. Crawley's neighbor,—Mr. Crawley the curate in Trollope's "Last Chronicles of Barset,"—who met him bowed with misery, and, simple and rough of speech, said to him for the strengthening of his heart, "It's dogged as does it." Confucius was of the same opinion twenty-five centuries ago when he said, "The man who lays one shovelful of earth upon the ground *and goes on*, that man is building the mountain"; and Lowell joins the chorus in his great poem of Columbus, worth all the poetry that our Columbian anniversary inspired, telling us that

> " Endurance is the crowning quality,
>   And patience all the passion of great hearts."

I like these many variations of a single theme. Their variety and the wide extent of time and space from which they come suggest the soundness of the lesson which they teach. There is another variation that by a long way round will bring me home to my continuing city which I have had in sight from every milestone of the way. It is the saying of General Grant's father when the general was on the way to Richmond and had been for a long time. " I think Ulysses will get there," said the old man, "for when he was a boy he had the gift of continuance." The gift of continuance is that which captures Richmond every time ; captures the thing desired, the craftsman's skill, the scholar's learning, the merchant's tact, the artist's power, the statesman's mastery. It is that which captures the continuing city, the unity of character which binds in one the hopes and aspirations of our youth and the attainments of our maturer years.

It is so with little things as well as with the enterprises of great pith and moment. Talking with my father not very long before his death about an experiment in business which he made in 1854, and did not make it go, and tried again in 1869 with better luck, I asked him, "Why did you do better the second time?" and he said: "Why, don't you see? *I held on.*" Three simple words, but they would tell the story of thousands and ten thousands who having the gift of continuance came at length unto their desired haven. As I read the biography of greatness, it is not the rule but the exception that the continuing city of its excellence and fame and influence comes like an exhalation of the dawn. It is built up stone by stone of slow, sweet patience and unconquerable hope, the foundations deep down out of sight where it is damp and chill and liker to a grave than to a pedestal or throne. The men of sudden reputation do not come to stay. In Tom Paine's happy and immortal phrase, they go up like a rocket and come down like the stick. Patiently and long the truly great ones struggle against odds, and make themselves of no reputation because they will not be disobedient to the heavenly vision. Sometimes the reputation never comes till they are gone, and

> " The hooting mob of yesterday in silent awe return
> To glean up the scattered ashes into History's golden urn."

Sometimes it lights their dying eyes with a bright momentary gleam. But that does not matter much. They have held on, they have had the gift of continuance, they have laid the first shovelful upon the earth and *have gone on;* they have been constant to their ideal, they have not disobeyed the heavenly vision, they have endured unto the end and they have been saved from weakness, vacillation, littleness of soul. And theirs is the continuing city, a life not fragmentary or dualistic, but mastered from the beginning to the end by the same constant inspiration.

"This is all well enough," I seem to hear you say, "for the elect, the mighty ones of genius, power, and fame. Such are not we." Yea, verily, and yet the power which rounds the pebble rounds the sphere. There is one gravitation only of the stars and aerolites, and the apple falling into Newton's mind to trouble it (as if it were the angel of Bethesda's pool) with some strange and secret charm. The gift of continuance is not the possession of a favored few: it is the possession of great multitudes of men and women. Their lives are narrow, meagre, hard. The temptation to give over the conflict often comes to them in the pauses of labor, in the night watches. But they do not yield to it. They hold on. They endure unto the end. And so doing the freedom of the continuing city is made theirs as absolutely as a Corot's or Millet's or Beethoven's, a Raphael's or Garrison's or Darwin's. And here, once more, let me remind you that we are too apt to underrate the moral quality of a man's regular vocation, his daily task, his business, to look somewhere apart from this for his opportunity for achieving character and doing good. But there is nothing else that is so determinative of a man's character, nothing else that so furnishes hands for his beneficence, and feet to run his errands of good will. Here is the scene of his temptations, ruinous for the weak, but to the strong new strength, making true the imagination of the savage warrior that the energy of the enemy he conquers is straightway added to his own. Here is the school of virtue, the gymnasium where it must run and wrestle, and find out its ability to stand up and resist when stoutly buffeted. As there is a statue in every block of marble, so in every enterprise of honest work for every man or woman there is an image of some goodliness of character, not to be liberated without many a well-directed blow. As you go about in these great cities you find all sorts of business going on. But it turns out that one great co-operative enterprise includes them all.

They are all making *men*, and sometimes the human speci-
mens turned out are cheaper than the wares; and then
again they shame the sculptor's statues and the worth of
precious stones.

I could speak of these hard times, hardly beginning yet to
better, and of the opportunity which they afford for making
or unmaking men. And yet I am inclined to think that,
after all, it is not the financial crisis, nor the long, slow,
up-hill work that follows it that is most trying to the stuff of
which the business man is made. These bring with them a
certain courage of their own, an *esprit de corps* that helps the
individual to pull himself together. Then all are in one boat,
or they are all "companions on a desert waste who share the
same dire thirst and therefore share the scanty water." It is
the continuity of life that tests the continuity of character,
"the same dull round" and common task each day renewed,
year after year, each unromantic, undramatic as the last.
In the parable of the sower, you will remember that there
was certain seed which started well enough; but when the
sun was up it was scorched, and because it had no root it
withered away. Is there nothing in this figure corresponding to the facts of modern business life? If so, why is it
that we have so many disappointments in the business and
social world; so many instances of men of whom we have
expected nothing but good and who have done nothing that
we know unworthy, suddenly unmasking and revealing to
us a vicious or a criminal countenance? I use a doubtful
figure; for it suggests that all along the man has been different from our imagination, and generally that is not true.
But the sun is up,— the hot blaze of manhood, so different
from its dewy morning hours, when everything was fresh and
glistering in an ideal and rosy light. And how many men
there are that have no root of personal conviction; only a
few flat and silly fibres spreading out into the surface-soil
of habit and conventionality; no root that strikes deep
down into earth where it may twine and twist itself about
some bowlder of conscience, of duty, of social loyalty, and

so be honor-bound and able to defy whatever winds may blow! There are men who are so happily endowed, who have such native strength of will, or whose early circumstances have so welded it, that they do not know the meaning of temptation. They can look upon the wine when it is red, or the gold when it is yellow, or the beauty of forbidden things when it is warm and palpitant, with an equal freedom from all base desire. There are those less favored at the start whom circumstances so befriend that they as little know the meaning of temptation. Either they have all they want or the more liberal allowance is not forced on their imagination with a persistency that shreds away their moorings to the good and true. But there are also those who, with the poorer outfit, also have the strain and fret of a continual temptation working on their lives. A hundred or a thousand times perhaps they have resisted before they have succumbed. There are men without fleck or stain whose whole lives long have not shown a half, a tenth, the energy of resistance that have some others which have gone to utter wreck. These tire of the perpetual struggle. They have given honesty a fair trial, and if it has been the best policy for them it has not been a money-making one. There are those who have tried some other and they have done much better, by the world's standards of success. Why not go after them? Besides, to many men midway of their career there comes, it would appear, a certain slackening of energy, impatience with life's humdrum quality, and the desire for change, that mean for them an anxious, dangerous time.

Some there are — the most, thank God — who can rally the good in the depths of their own natures, fortify themselves with precious memories and lofty hopes, and so get past the strait 'twixt Scylla and Charybdis into calm seas beyond. Some are less fortunate. Moreover, in the sphere of talent, we see that no man can afford to be content with any past attainment. To do as well as he has done, he must do better. As the old sculptor said to the young

one, he must get his second wind. The fable of Narcissus
is a fable which the history of art continually makes good,—
the tragedy of self-admiration. Hence, self-imitation, repe-
tition. Certainly, Cazin's pictures are very lovely. But
have you not a fear that once too often he may repeat the
beauty of that evening sky? When Pygmalion fell in love
with his own workmanship it was granted life. But that
was an exception. Death is the general consequence of
the artist's satisfaction with his statue, picture, poem, score.
And as in art, so in life : the common tragedy is the self-
content which poisons good desire ; the sinking down, the
falling back upon the thing achieved, upon the goal attained,
and so inevitably falling below that and short of it as time
goes on. *We must do better than we have done or we cannot
do as well.*

Time was when the ideal conception of the preacher was
"a youth of folly, an old age of cares,"—of pious cares, pre-
sumably, redressing the eternal scales and making the bad
fly up, the good remain below. But what the poet wrote
was different, "A youth of frolics, an old age of cards,"— a
likelier sequence than the other. But even if the ideal of
sainthood or the ideal of the novelist,— wild oats and then a
crop of orange blossoms and the wide respect which money
always wins,— could be generally realized, what nobler
spirit would not sympathize with Martineau's contempt for
a life in two volumes : the first a jest-book, and the second
a mixture of the satire and the liturgy? Were the second a
cash-book or a religious novel, would it be any better? No ;
let us have the whole life of a piece, from youth to age one
constant inspiration of nobility and truth and kindliness and
earnestness and peace and love. No fear that such an inspiration would entail the loss of any joy of youth on which
maturity could look back without regret. There have been
thousands who have dwelt in this continuing city, and left
untasted never a joy that is the proper food of any healthy
boy or girl, never a satisfaction in which a noble youth or
maid could take unqualified delight. And the most persua-

sive argument for such a constant inspiration is the spectacle of a life obedient to its sacred law.

"We have here no continuing city," said the New Testament writer, "but we seek one to come." We have one here, and more than one,— the City of Unbroken Time, the City of Organic Evolution, and the City of Persistent Character, wherein all those do dwell who keep from youth to age one purpose strong, one steadfast, high intent to learn those things that are true and do those things that are right. Yet here so trebly rich we still can say with the New Testament writer, "We seek one to come." And never more eagerly than when such men as we have known, inhabitants of the continuing city, obedient to its laws, are taken from our sight. We cannot make them dead. Somehow, somewhere, we feel, and seem to know, they must be living still, "in other kingdoms of a sweeter air." However that may be, the central fact remains that here and now

> "There is a city builded by no hand,
> And unapproachable by sea or shore,
> And unassailable by any band
> Of storming soldiery forevermore."

THE OLD TESTAMENT AND THE
HIGHER CRITICISM.

In the first place, what is the Higher Criticism? It is
an attempt to view the different parts of the Bible in a large
and general way, to discover when the different books were
written, and, if possible, by whom they were written (though
this particular is generally of much less importance than
the other); and, yet further, their relations to each other
and to the various times in which they were produced,—
how they were influenced by these, and what influence
they had upon them,— if, haply, in this way the line of
evolution may be traced from the beginning to the end of
that millennium which, speaking roughly, synchronized with
the production of the Bible from its earliest to its latest
parts,— from the ninth century B.C. to the second after and
inclusive. I say "speaking roughly," because, no doubt,
there are fragments inhering in the Old Testament books
which come down from a greater antiquity than the ninth
century B.C. Twelve hundred years would cover the development of English literature from Cædmon and Bæda, its
earliest beginners, to Watson and Kipling, the latest of the
long and honorable line. A similar period would cover
nearly or quite everything in the Bible, the earliest fragments which are imbedded in the histories and other books
included. Hence the rank absurdity of thinking or speaking
of the Bible as if it were one book. It is a compendium of
Jewish literature until the end of the second Christian century. The sixty-six books which this compendium contains
do not begin to tell the number of the authors who took

---

* To be followed by a sermon on the New Testament.

part in their composition; for there were, probably, scores of writers implicated in the production of the Psalms and Proverbs, and many more in the composition of the prophets than appears upon their face.

To speak of the Higher Criticism seems to imply a lower. It does,— a lower and a lowest. The lower criticism of the Bible is that which is merely textual. Of course, this and the Higher Criticism often play into each other's hands : the age of the book and the circumstances of its production help us to understand the individual texts, and the individual texts help us to understand the age and character of the books in which they appear. The Higher Criticism takes up into itself almost bodily the lower textual criticism, but is as much more than that as a man is more than the food which he consumes. It is one of the loveliest ironies of man's intellectual history that the superstitious reverence for the Bible has contributed immensely to the demonstration of its natural genesis and human character. Its text never would have received the attention which it has received if it had not been regarded as a sacred text. Every line has been interrogated, every word. And all this work has been the getting out of material for the Higher Criticism to work with in its day. Indeed, some of the most important elements of the Higher Criticism have been developed by the lower textual criticism, which said, " I will water my garden bed "; and, lo ! "its brook became a river, and the river a sea."

There is a much lower criticism than that of the merely textual critic. It is that of the dogmatic critic, subjecting the Bible to the necessities of his particular system of theology. In this business there has been much bullying of the witnesses, much putting of them on the rack. Texts have had a meaning tortured out of them, agreeable to the wishes of the dogmatist. But the violence done has been for the most part unconscious. Because unconscious, it has been no less miserable in its effects. Beautiful as is our King James translation, it fairly reeks with the theological preconceptions of the translators,— so much so that a great linguist declared not long ago that to retranslate the Bible would be to revolutionize the religion of the English-speaking world. Yet even more perversive of the meaning of the Bible than its translation has been its theological interpretation, the reading into it of all sorts and conditions of theological and ecclesiastical ideas.

Criticism, strictly speaking, is judgment; and hence the so-called criticism of the dogmatic theologian hunting up proof texts for his dogmas is not criticism at all. It is advocacy, and as unlike the true criticism as the advocacy of the lawyer for his client is unlike the judgment of the judge upon the bench. And still we have not reached the lowest deep. That is the so-called criticism of the wilful and deliberate depreciator of the Bible. This is criticism in the vulgar sense of those to whom all criticism is identical with fault-finding and depreciation. There are even clergymen who have not unlearned this childish notion. Said one of them, speaking of Dr. Briggs, "That he or any one should presume to criticise the word of God!" But we have plenty of what is called criticism which is nothing but deliberate depreciation. It revels in "the mistakes of Moses," unaware that the Higher Criticism finds but "ten words" of Moses in the Old Testament (if so many),— the Ten Commandments, which, in their simplest form, are possibly from that great leader's shaping hand.

Having thus distinguished between the Higher Criticism and certain lower forms, let me, in the next place, remind you that the Higher Criticism is not something new. You would imagine it to be so from the way many people talk of late in our city, where a distinguished clergyman has been putting out, in a very genial and fascinating way, some of the results of the Higher Criticism as it concerns the Old Testament. What he has done he has done very modestly and cautiously, sometimes with a strong accent of personal preference, as in his utterly uncritical idea that Job is the oldest whole book in the Bible. The leading scholars in our theological schools would seldom find his opinions unduly radical; much oftener unduly conservative and traditional. They are not new opinions. With one significant exception they were familiar to me in my Divinity School days; and my dear teacher, Dr. George R. Noyes, held them fifty years ago, in common with the most learned German scholars of his time, and the most learned English scholars also,— these, however, a much smaller company. Some of the most important of these results were clearly and irrefragably developed early in the present century, the documentary character of the Penta-teuch earlier by half a century. Even the newest of Dr. Abbott's critical conclusions, which — the late origin of the priestly portions of the Pentateuch — is more central to the Higher Criticism of the Old Testament than any other,— even this conclusion had its "seeds and weak beginnings" sixty years ago in the simultaneous but mutually isolated intui-tions of Reuss and Vatke, was clearly indicated by Graf in 1866, and splendidly developed by Kuenen in 1869, from which time its conquests were as rapid as those of the Dar-winian biology. I cannot but be just a little proud that I appropriated this conclusion with enthusiasm twenty years ago, and made it central to my lectures on the Old Testa-ment given in 1877, and that my book, "The Bible of To-day," was the first book published in America (1878) expository of a critical idea which was destined to be as fertile in Old Testament matters as Darwin's natural selec-tion in biology.

No, the conclusions of the Higher Criticism are not new. The surprising thing is that they should seem so to so many persons in this community. Where have they been? What have they been reading? One thing is sure: a good many of the clergy know how little novelty there is in them. They know that they are taught in many of their theological schools, and taught there with all possible reverence and sobriety. There could not be anything more foolish and absurd than the industrious circulation of the idea that there is something of enmity to the Bible in the Higher Criticism. The most tender of the saints have not studied the Bible more reverently than the most revolutionary critics. These have been not only reverent of the Bible, but of the truth. They have only accepted results that have been forced upon them by the onset of the facts in irresistible array. If the field had been an open one, unfortressed by traditional prejudices and opinions of the most impregnable character, they would not have held out so long. But there has been this advantage in the situation : obliged, because of traditional prejudices and opinions, to give ten reasons for each onward step where one would have been sufficient but for those prejudices and opinions, their advance, if much slower than it would otherwise have been, has been much more incontrovertible, much more incontestably assured.

The method of the Higher Criticism has been the method of science. Beginning with what is most surely known, it has slowly and cautiously worked out its way from that into the adjacent region, and then into the regions more and more remote. In the Old Testament the most authentic writings of the prophets have been the starting-point. The most obvious outcome of this process, availing itself of whatever helps the narrower criticism of texts and separate books could furnish, is the negation and destruction of a great many traditional conceptions as to the age and authorship of the various books. Taking the Old Testament books in their traditional English order, which is not altogether that of the Jewish and other early versions, we are assured that Moses did not write the Pentateuch nor Joshua the book which bears his name, nor David the Psalms ascribed to him in their headings, nor Solomon the Proverbs or Ecclesiastes or Solomon's Song ; that Isaiah wrote only about one-third of the book which bears his name ; Jeremiah, less than the whole of that ascribed to him and no part of Lamentations ; Daniel, the prophet of the captivity, not a syllable of the book ascribed to him ; Zechariah, a part only of the book called Zechariah's.

With these negations of traditional authorship, which by no means represent the full amount, there have been as many, if not more, of dates traditionally assigned, as of the Pentateuch to the fifteenth century B.C., and Job to a much older date, to which Dr. Abbott fondly clings; of the Psalms to David's and the immediately succeeding time; of the books ascribed to Solomon to this time; the book of Daniel to later years of the captivity in the sixth century; and so on. There has been a movement forward all along the line, but a few centuries here and many there, only a few of the thirty-nine Old Testament books even approximating to the dates assigned to them in the traditional chronology. To go into particulars would be to pass from the negative to the positive aspect of the matter, and I wish to give the former all its naked force.

If these negations of dates and authorship traditionally assigned to the Old Testament books were all the Higher Criticism had to show, it would deserve the contumely heaped upon it by its more violent opponents, and the indifference or distrust of all whose spiritual appetite demands something more than a Barmecide feast of negative conclusions, empty of all traditional dates and personal associations. But even the negations of the Higher Criticism are not so barren as they might be, by a great deal. They are a notation by which very real values are expressed. They carry in their train a host of positive results as much more interesting and impressive, as they are in themselves, as are the movements of the heavens more interesting and impressive than the algebraic x by which their unknown quantities may be expressed.

For example: the main interest of the Old Testament criticism has centred in that set of five books, the first five in our Bibles as commonly published, which is called the Pentateuch. Now what proportion do the results attained concerning the Pentateuch bear to the mere negation of the Mosaic authorship? To say a hundred or a thousand to one would be no exaggeration, yet the criticism of the Pentateuch has been destructive of much more than its Mosaic authorship. It has destroyed the unity of its composition.

It has made Deuteronomy, the fifth section of the fivefold Pentateuch, a book by itself, dating from the last quarter of the seventh century B.C., when Moses was some seven centuries dead. The four preceding books the critics have broken up into, first, an early set of laws, the " Book of Covenants," which you will find in Exodus xxi.-xxiii. 19 ; second, a document in which Elohim is the name used for God ; third, a document in which Jehovah is the name used for God ; fourth, a document fusing these ; fifth, a priestly code containing nearly all the priestly regulations of Exodus, Numbers, and Leviticus, which was not fairly published until Moses had been dead about nine centuries, — all these parts being fused together with Deuteronomy and Joshua at a still later date, forming a Hexateuch, a sixfold book, which, and not the Pentateuch, is the true compound unit of the earlier Hebrew history. All this is destructive criticism, certainly. But it is the same kind of destruction which goes on when an incongruous heap of stone and iron and lumber is sorted and selected and used for building a house, most solid and symmetrical, fit shelter of a living, loving home.

If we could have the Hexateuch arranged for ordinary reading as it has been in the ideal constructions of the critics, it would have all the advantage over the present arrangement that a noble building has over the raw materials from which it is made. Thanks to the constructive genius of the Higher Criticism, a unity that was merely one of clumsy aggregation has become vital and organic. Every separate part is vitally related to some stage of Israel's growth in spiritual things. It reflects a changing civilization, a deeper ethical and relig-ious consciousness, as we pass from the Book of Covenants, a product of the ninth century B.C., to the Prophetic Narra-tives, called the Jehovistic document, the story book of which we never tire ; next to the Elohistic document ; then to the fusion of the two, with added parts, — all this eighth-century work ; then to Deuteronomy (621 B.C.) and a revision of the parts already named in the Deuteronomic — i.e., half priestly, half prophetic—spirit ; and, finally, in the fifth century B.C., to the Priestly Code, and the grand fusion of this with all the rest, and the re-editing of the whole which, in the third or fourth century, brought the Pentateuch and Joshua into their present shape, twelve centuries later than the popular imagination has conceived.

Nor do the constructive achievements of the Higher Criticism end with the rearrangement of the Hexateuch, even as far as the Hexateuch is concerned. The order thus discovered is that of a great army, which, as it goes marching on, sweeps into its files the wavering swarms of national allies and bordering states, and makes them energetic and consenting parts of its own unitary force and might. The critical rearrangement of the Hexateuch, far from ending with itself, furnishes a unifying principle of Old Testament relations, which brings the books of Samuel and Kings and Chronicles and the prophetic books in their true chronological order, the Psalms and other writings, such as Ruth, Jonah, Proverbs, into harmonious alliance with the Hexateuch, corresponding with and illustrating one part or another of its composite unity.

Thus it appears that the books of Samuel and Kings fall into line with those portions of the Pentateuch which are strongly marked by the prophetic spirit, the prophets Amos and Hosea, Isaiah and Micah, at the same time into the same line. Not without real critical insight did the Jews call the books of Samuel and Kings "the Early Prophets," so strong in them is the spirit of the eighth-century prophets, the first who left a written record of their prophecies.* But Jeremiah's place is with the Deuteronomist, so much so that some have imagined Deuteronomy to be his work, as part prophet and part priest doing his best to reconcile discordant elements ; and Ezekiel is significant of that more priestly tendency which culminated in the Priestly Code after the return of the captive Israelites from Babylon where the

* It should be understood that *all* pre-exilic writings were much edited and altered after the exile

priestly code was worked out, not without much ingenious and affectionate inclusion of such ritual forms as had been generally in use or had fallen into innocuous desuetude in the hurly-burly of invasion and expatriation.

The Psalmists who are many, equally with the Prophets, bring their glory and honor into the evolution of the Hexateuch. The most of their Psalms are nothing more nor less than the echoes of the law in the hearts of the people ; and the collection has been very properly called the Hymn-book of the Second Temple, the temple built after the captivity and finished about 516 B.C. Thus all, or nearly all, of them are assigned to a time from five hundred to nine hundred years after the time of David, to whom the most searching criticism allows no part or lot in them whatever. But, if it is a little matter thus to determine their chronological relations, it is not a little matter that by this determination they become to us the voice of a great congregation, and not merely the unreal pietism of a semi-barbarous and immoral king. It is not a little matter that to the priests, whom we have habitually depreciated or despised in comparison with the prophets, we are most indebted for those parts of the Old Testament which have made it precious to innumerable hearts. To the same priests we owe the books of Chronicles and Ezra and Nehemiah, as history prejudiced and imperfect, but as memoirs of their times, the third and fourth centuries B.C., most serviceable to the historians of those times, who are now endeavoring to pluck out the heart of their mystery. These books are on the best of terms with the priestly portions and the last editions of the Pentateuch, as also are the first part of Zechariah (chapters i.-viii.) and Malachi, the last book in the popular Old Testament; while the books of Jonah and Ruth are in spirited rebellion against the narrow and exclusive policy of those who would shut Israel up in selfish isolation.

In the development of this progressive relation of so many books to the evolution of the Hexateuch we have a constructive achievement even greater than the rearrangement

of the Hexateuch. It substitutes for a purely mechanical
and irrational arrangement of the Old Testament material
such a relation and connection that we can say,

> " Mark how one string, sweet husband to another,
>   Strikes each in each by mutual ordering."

Immeasurable the gain of every part in interest, in vitality,
in historical and spiritual significance. And there are many
incidental gains which are of great importance. What a
gain, for instance, to the character of God, to find that Deuteronomy is no authentic revelation of his character and purposes, but a magnificent literary *tour de force* to effect a
compromise of diverse religious elements ! The character of
the Hebrew people makes an equal gain when the slaughter
of the Canaanites, for which such lame excuses have been
made, and which has often furnished terrible instructions to
fanatical religionists, is remanded to the ideal sphere : some
pious soul so dreamed what ought to be, but never altogether
had his way. Another incidental gain is in the matter of
Isaiah. The criticism which makes chapters xl.–lxvi. a separate prophecy, two centuries later than the rest, leaves to the
prophet Isaiah all that he needs for his imperishable fame.
The later portion gives us another prophet equal to, if not
greater than, Isaiah, singing "the Lord's song in a strange
land," singing it with the pathos and the passion of a captive
Jew rejoicing in the prospect of his people's going back to
rebuild the waste places of Jerusalem. We have a similar
gain when the book of Daniel is transferred from the sixth
century B.C. to the second, where it becomes the expression
of that passion of revolt against the tyranny of Antiochus
Epiphanes which raised the standard of the heroic Maccabees, and carried it to victory. If it is any loss to have even
a criticism so conservative as that of Dr. Driver detach the
Psalms entirely from King David, surely, the gain is infi-

---

* Cheyne, Duhm, and others argue convincingly that the Second Isaiah ends with
chapter lv. and that the remaining chapters are a series of different prophecies, mainly
from the time of Nehemiah, about 432 B.C.

nitely greater which interprets them as the growth of several later centuries. As much as ever they contain

> " Words that have drunk transcendent meaning up
> From the best passion of all bygone times,
> Steeped through with tears of triumph or remorse,
> Sweet with all sainthood, cleansed with martyr fires,"

though not unmixed with baser elements. Henceforth they are the spiritual biography of Israel for five hundred years, with here and there an accent so purely personal that we feel as if we ought to veil our faces from the agony and contrition of a troubled soul. As the name of David became the centre of aggregation for the hymns and spiritual songs of Israel, so did Solomon's name for its proverbial wisdom and pessimistic philosophy, and the name of Job for the long debate concerning the misfortunes and the sufferings of righteous men. In every case the gain is large which makes the individual wither, while the race is more and more. How grandly, too, the Higher Criticism has rescued the book of Jonah and the Song of Songs from the contempt of vulgar literalists and the qualms of prurient prudes (the latter no less from the stuff and nonsense of allegorical interpretation), and set them both on high as worthy of all honor,— the one for its catholic sympathy with alien peoples, and the other from its praise of simple, faithful love, so radiantly beautiful and so passionately pure !

But these incidental gains, to which indefinite additions might easily be made, must not detain us from that larger synthesis which is involved in the gradual evolution of the Hexateuch and the other books that correspond to the successive stages of its development, which was a business of some five centuries' duration. The positive, constructive achievement, *par excellence*, of the Higher Criticism within the Old Testament limits is the history of a national religious evolution from a fetichism or totemism deifying trees and stones to the worship of one God, not of and for Israel alone, but of the universe, and, if through Israel, for all

mankind. From an original fetich worship, safely con-
jectured from the survivals of a later time, Israel in Egypt
went forward to the worship of great natural forms and
forces, and principally to the worship of a dreadful god of
fire, much like the Ammonitish Molech and the Moabitish
Chemosh, whose worship was with human sacrifices and
other cruel rites.

This god would seem to have been worshipped under different names, one of them Yahweh, as nearly as we can
make out; or there were different gods from which the one
called Yahweh came uppermost in course of time. It would
also appear that Moses was influential in effecting his as-
cendency, perhaps, and likely enough, because Yahweh was
the god of his own tribe. The name matters little. What
does matter is that Moses connected the worship of this
Yahweh with morality in the Ten Commandments, not as
we have them now, but much more simply and somewhat
differently; for Moses was no monotheist, and did not object to the idolatrous worship of Yahweh, however it may
superficially appear in the Old Testament narratives. (As
George Washington in his later life set out to make over
his early correspondence, so Israel, growing older, set out
to revise its early records; and no pre-exilic writings have
come down to us in their integrity. Eternal vigilance is the
price of critical accuracy and a real knowledge of the early
world.) From the time of Moses to that of Hosea, the
eighth-century prophet, availing ourselves of every possible
check and countercheck, we make out that for these five
hundred years monolatry, the worship of one god, without
denying the existence or the power of other gods, was Israel's loftiest ideal, too lofty for common or habitual realization.

The worship of other gods with Yahweh was commoner
than his exclusive worship. Witness the Baal worship of
the northern tribes, and the motley worship of Kings Solomon, Ahaz, and Manasseh. In the eighth century B.C. Israel, for the first time, under the lead of such great prophets

as Isaiah and Micah, arrived at the purely monotheistic idea that there was only one God, that he was to be worshipped without any image, that he was a righteous God, and was rightly worshipped not by sacrifices, but by the righteousness of his people. Only a small minority were ready for so high a truth. A century later there was a compromise, the details of which are to be found in Deuteronomy. It was substantially that the true worship of Yahweh consisted of sacrifices and righteousness, only the sacrifices must be offered in Jerusalem, and there only. This was a prudential measure to prevent the idolatrous worship of Yahweh or the worship of other gods. The violent revolution by which this compromise was enforced was soon followed by the Babylonian captivity, a period of intense literary activity, whose most signal fruit was the Priestly Code, the Levitical legislation of the Hexateuch, which is most prominent and exclusive of other matter in Leviticus. Not amid the thunders of Sinai, but by the waters of Babylon, was the law in its full sense delivered, and not to Moses, but to some school of daring innovators and editors working very quietly, lest they should undo their shrewd and patient toil.

With much bold invention there was no doubt much of liberal appropriation and the freest handling imaginable of venerable documents. The compromise of Deuteronomy had come full circle. There the priests had the best of it: here they had everything their own way. But the religious evolution still went on. A loftier spirituality, a more inward righteousness. is witnessed by the later Psalms and other writings of the centuries that bring us forward to the beginning of the Christian era.

This meagre outline is almost a travesty of that history of Israel's religious evolution which the Higher Criticism has achieved. Can these dry bones live? They can and do under the magic spell of the great master critics, such as Kuenen and Wellhausen and Cheyne, and our own faithful and courageous Toy. Touched by their hands, they are clothed upon straightway with palpitating flesh: their blood is warm with human love and hate and hope and fear and joy. And the history so made alive, as compared with the mechanical traditional scheme of Israel's general decadence from, and spasmodic efforts to regain, the heights of an original supernatural revelation, is full of a superb reality and an incalculable interest and inspiration.

There is one negative aspect of this matter which I have not touched. And some will say that, whatever compensation there may be for the particular negations indicated heretofore, there is no compensation for the general negation which I have in mind,— the negation of the claim made for the Old Testament, that it is a book of supernatural inspiration. This claim is not abandoned entirely, however modified, by some whose honorable rank among the higher critics is assured. Canon Driver, the English Churchman, who would assent to almost every proposition I have set forth, tells us that neither the inspiration nor authority of the Old Testament is affected by these critical results. True enough, if the measure of inspiration and authority is the ability of any speech or writing to inspire us and to bind our wills in loyal service of the truth as recognized and known, but utterly and miserably false, if what is meant is that the old-time doctrines of inspiration and authority emerge from the seven-times-heated furnace of the modern critic with their feet unscarred. They are shrivelled, and they turn to ashes in its steady flame. And why not? There is no claim in the Old Testament for the special supernatural inspiration of its various parts. If individual writers thought themselves supernaturally inspired, that only means that their psychology was primitive, naïve. None of the individual writers knew of the Old Testament as a whole. The older writers, of course, knew nothing of the later parts; the later writers, little or nothing of those contemporaneous with their own. The older writings had for them no supernatural character. If they had, how could they hack about among them so freely, adding here, subtracting there, as certainly they did?

The formation of the Old Testament set of books was very gradual, a process covering some eight hundred years and involving many doubts and uncertainties even among those who were most influential in the matter. The doubts and uncertainties would have been multiplied indefinitely if the compilers had imagined they were making up a list of inspired books in our traditional sense, but they imagined nothing of the sort. The belief in supernatural inspiration and authority was a gradual development; and there was nothing in the process of its growth to commend it to an intelligent mind, nor to any one not bound to stultify himself at any cost. To read and understand the natural history of the Old Testament as the Higher Criticism has developed it, and still cling to any theory, however attenuated, of its supernatural inspiration, is more irrational and absurd than to believe in the Ptolemaic astronomy, in full view of all that the astronomers have taught us since Copernicus.

But the negation of the supernatual inspiration of the Old Testament is but the open portal to a large and noble affirmation. Anti-supernaturalism, like godliness, with contentment, is great gain. Great gain for God, whom it relieves of many monstrous imputations. Great gain for those who wrote the several books, no longer seen as puppets, but as living, thinking men, tempted in all things just as we are, and not always without sin. Great gain for us, in that we are no longer bound to justify everything contained in the Old Testament, but can doubt and deny on the same grounds as in other literature; and because, moreover, by the negation of the supernaturally sacred character of the Old Testament the scope of sacred literature is indefinitely increased, and we find its great examples wherever there is anything written by any man or woman that thrills us with the touch of truth or beauty, that wakens us to nobler aspirations, that comforts and sustains us in the sorrows and anxieties which are inseparable from the discipline and progress of our mortal life.

THE NEW TESTAMENT AND THE
HIGHER CRITICISM.*

In popular apprehension, which corresponds to the traditional chronology, there is a gulf of some four centuries and
a half between the last book of the Old Testament and the
first book of the New. The idea of this gulf has been
wonderfully effective in perpetuating the idea that Jesus was
"a high priest after the order of Melchizedek"; that is to
say, without historical antecedents, a man unrelated to the
development of his time and race. Now one of the most
significant achievements of the Higher Criticism has been
to bridge this gulf, partly with material brought forward
from the Old Testament, partly with material from the
Apocrypha, and partly with material from sources wholly
external to the Bible and Apocrypha. The consequence is
that the gulf between Malachi and Matthew has been not
merely bridged, but filled in with a mass of literature which
makes the passage of this period as secure as that of any
period in either Testament. Moreover, the wilderness has
been made to blossom like the rose; for the quality of the
literature to which these centuries, formerly a blank, gave
birth is not surpassed by any in the Old Testament. Its
mass includes the majority of the Psalms and Proverbs, the
splendid prophecy of Joel, the best part of Zechariah, the
immensely interesting book of Daniel, Ecclesiastes, Esther,
Solomon's Song, and Chronicles with their appendices, Ezra
and Nehemiah. It also includes the whole of the Apocrypha, some books of which surely are not unworthy to be
bound up with the best books of the Old Testament or New.
It is only the madness of inveterate prejudice that does not

* Preceded by a sermon on the Old Testament.

find the Wisdom of Solomon superior to Ecclesiastes or the first book of Maccabees superior to Esther. The Prayer of Manasses is interesting as an early form of the fictitious death-bed repentance of the famous infidel, the delightful book of Tobit as a counterblast to the book of Job. Beyond the verge of the Apocrypha, we have such books as the Apocalypse of Enoch and the Psalms of Solomon and the Sibylline Books, all, with the rest, of great importance in making clear the line of evolution from Malachi to Matthew. With such a gulf as formerly opened here, the supernatural origin of Christianity was an almost inevitable hypothesis ; but, with that gulf filled in as it has been by the Higher Criticism, a rose upon its stem is not more natural than was Jesus with his gospel of compassion and his Messianic consciousness at the time when he appeared.

Coming now to the New Testament, it must be confessed that in many instances the representatives of the Higher Criticism have not dealt with it with the same sincerity and courage they have brought to the Old. "The reason, of course, is obvious," says Dr. Gore, one of the principal authors of the book called "Lux Mundi," a volume of English High Church contributions to current problems of criticism and theology,—"the reason is obvious why what can be admitted in the Old Testament could not, without results disastrous to the creed, be admitted in the New." Even a critic so free as Cheyne, in his Old Testament dealings, proposes to make the safety of the Church's creed a factor in the decision of New Testament questions.

All this is very natural. Turn the thing about, and you will find counter-illustrations of the same disposition. My dear friend, Rabbi Gottheil, is much more easily disposed to radical conclusions in the criticism of the New Testament than of the Old. But the value of evidence is not in the least affected by the magnitude of the issues at stake. The evidence that would justify a certain conclusion concerning the Old Testament will justify a similar conclusion concerning the New Testament. The Higher Criticism has only one method, the method of science in dealing with all documents in or beyond the Bible's liberal scope. Honestly adhering to this method, we arrive, first of all in the New Testament as in the Old, at certain negative results. Here, as there, the movement forward of the various books from their traditional anchorage has been strongly marked, though not without occasional recessions. These recessions have been rejoiced over by the conservative and apologetic critics with exceeding great joy and some hilarity. Andrews Norton, in his "Genuineness of the Gospels," broke down the criticism of Eichhorn, which assigned them to the last decades of the second century; and the admiring followers of F. C. Baur have conceded that the Gospels reached their present form from twenty-five to fifty years earlier than that giant among critics confidently believed and taught.

But these movements backward of the tide leave the traditional conceptions of the character of the New Testament as effectually stranded as before, if not quite so high up the beach. As the case now stands, we have the Synoptic (the first three) Gospels assigned to the last quarter of the present century; Luke and Matthew, possibly, beyond; the Fourth Gospel to the first quarter of the second century or a somewhat later time; Acts, also to a date a good deal forward from its traditional date to 100 to 120 A.D.; the Pastoral Epistles (to Timothy and Titus), to a much and Ephesians to a somewhat later date than that of Paul's; the Epistles ascribed to Peter, to times long after his death, the first to the first quarter of the second century, and the second to the third or fourth. It is evident at a glance that these changes of New Testament dates involve many changes of authorship. Of negative conclusions the maximum of certainty as concerns the Epistles commonly ascribed to Paul is that he did not write the Epistle to the Hebrews: it is quite certain that he did not write the Epistles to Timothy and Titus and the Ephesians; also that John did not write the Apocalypse, nor Peter and John the Epistles that bear their names, nor Matthew, Mark, and Luke the first

three Gospels in their present form, nor John the Fourth
Gospel in any valid sense. Closely affiliated with these
negative results there are grave doubts as to the authorship
of other books,— the James Epistle and the Pauline * Epistles
to the Philippians and Colossians.

Slight, indeed, would be the gratitude that we should owe
to the Higher Criticism of the New Testament if the results
already named were all it has to show. But these results, so
purely or dominantly negative as I have presented them, are
but the obverse of a shield which on the other side is radiant with the glow of many positive results. Wide, from first
to last, has been the range of inference as to the priority of
one Gospel or another. Only Luke has never (?) been assigned
to the first place. John has been, and Matthew ; but now it
is almost or quite universally agreed among the critics of the
highest rank that the priority belongs to Mark, but whether
Luke or Matthew next is still in doubt. The allowances of the
most conservative critics and the revised opinions of the most
radical conduct us to the last quarter of the first century as
the anterior limit that includes all three of the Synoptics.

But the ground of interest in the New Testament that is
more attractive than any other, more fascinating and en-
grossing, is the Fourth Gospel. The interest attaching to
this Gospel has been hardly less central to New Testament
criticism than that attaching to the Pentateuch has been to
the Old. After much pushing backward and forward on the
smoky field, the fight seems nearly at an end, and the victory
to be with those denying the authorship of John. For thirty
years the tendency has been as strong this way as for twenty
years before (after the Rupert charge of Baur) it was the
other. The criticism of Baur, about 1845, was utterly hos-
tile to John's authorship of the Gospel, and assigned it to a
date so far advanced toward the end of the second century
as 170 A.D. The reaction from this position was most strenuous, and the tide was increasingly favorable to John's authorship until Theodore Keim applied himself to the matter

---

* That is, developed on the lines of Paul's later speculation.

about thirty years ago. But the recession of the last thirty years toward the position of Baur has never brought us back to his exact position.

There came a time, in tunnelling Mont Cenis, when the workmen from one end heard the click of the tools which the workmen from the other end were driving into the great rocky wall. Something like this has happened in the criticism of the Fourth Gospel. We have had two parties working in opposite directions; but each has been obliged to make concessions by the changing fortunes of the great debate until, at last, we find them standing quite comfortably together on the common ground that the Fourth Gospel in its present form was written early in the second, or late in the first, quarter of the second century; that its long discourses are the parts furthest removed from the historic truth, and are no genuine reflections of the actual teachings of Jesus; that, nevertheless, there are elements of a genuine tradition in the Gospel, both of fact and phrase, which may have derived their impulse from the apostle John; and, more surely, from some authentic source. One of the great contentions concerning the Fourth Gospel has been as to whether Justin Martyr, writing about the middle of the second century, knew the Fourth Gospel. It is pretty certain that he did not know it, and very certain that he did not know it as John's. But, as the discussion has proceeded, this point has become of less importance.

There are still those who are not without hope that they can push this Gospel back to the beginning of the second century; and it is comical to see how eagerly any new discovery that seems to promise this result is seized upon, as if it were a hand to pluck up their drowning honor by the locks. The reason for this eagerness is that the Fourth Gospel represents the high-water mark of the progressive idealization of Jesus in the New Testament. Particularly notable is the way in which those called the progressive orthodox cling to the authenticity of John. Look through their books, and you will find them quoting him a dozen times where the Synoptics are quoted once. That is to say, they are building their toppling edifice of the super-human Jesus on the quicksand of the New Testament terri-tory. But an earlier date for this Gospel by some twenty or thirty years will not save its character as an authentic reproduction of the facts of Jesus' life. Professor Toy as-sures me that, could it, by any critical violence, be pushed back to the beginning of the second century, its character would remain the same : it would still be a dogmatic render-ing of the life of Jesus in terms of Greek philosophy, fore-shadowing the unethical character of the Nicene Creed in its avoidance of all ethical significance. I quoted this opin-ion to a professor in one of our most orthodox theological schools, and he assented to it heartily.

The utmost to which the greed of passionate conserva-tism is likely to attain is this : that the Fourth Gospel is a dogmatic treatise of the first quarter of the second century, holding imbedded in its unhistorical discourses a few golden grains of genuine tradition. And the gain to the natural, human Jesus from this conclusion will be in direct proportion to the loss to the traditional supernatural con-ception or any recent adumbration of that conception in the new orthodox theology.

The Higher Criticism has worked out not only the obvi-ous differences of the Synoptic Gospels from the Fourth, but also the resemblances and differences of the Synoptics among themselves. The resemblances are strongly marked, and point unmistakably to a common basis of traditional information. In fact, they are called the Synoptics (and their writers Synoptists), not because they present a synop-sis of the facts of Jesus' life, but because a synopsis can be made of the three narratives. Not only is the thread of the narrative the same in all three, but the general arrangement is the same. There are only about thirty verses in Mark which do not appear in Matthew or Luke. Forty like sec-tions appear in Matthew and Luke, and these have each twenty in common with Mark. Nevertheless there are, with the agreements and resemblances, differences which are extremely baffling, and which have led to many different renderings of their mutual relations and their relations to their common sources. Critics who place Mark first in order of time, generally place Matthew next, but not all of them. Evidently, in both Matthew and Mark there has been much working over and re-editing. We have here the same process of aggregation and redaction that obtained in the book-making of the Old Testament.

The matter which the Synoptics have in common has been called "The Triple Tradition"; and it is very interesting in that it contains a much simpler and less miraculous account of Jesus than the three Gospels in their entirety. This triple tradition brings us very close, no doubt, to the oral tradition that was most widely current among the followers of Jesus some forty years after his death. But we should by no means wish to limit ourselves to this common matter. Luke's additions to it are particularly precious, containing as they do, among other things, the story of the Good Samaritan and the parable of the Prodigal Son.

Passing from the Gospels to the Epistles, Paul's quadrilateral, impregnable even to the assault of F. C. Baur, is made up of Romans, the two Corinthians, and Galatians. Baur would allow none but these of the fourteen attributed to Paul to be authentic; but even those who have the greatest admiration for his genius have added to "the big four" First Thessalonians, Philippians, and Philemon, and, less confidently, Colossians. Taking these eight, we have in them the growth of Paul's ideal Jesus from a man in Thessalonians through the increasing grandeurs of Corinthians and Romans until, at length, in the Epistles to the Philippians and Colossians, he stands upon the utmost verge of super-angelic power and grace, where, but a step, and he has crossed the mystic line which divides him from the Eternal Logos of the Fourth Gospel.

As for the other six Epistles ascribed to Paul, in the New Testament headings and in popular belief, that to the

Hebrews is the most certainly not his of them all. It is a superb continuation of his thought in a manner very different from his, but with a genius equal to his own : from the literary standpoint, much superior. The pastoral Epistles to Timothy and Titus have been related to the developments and controversies of the second century. They may contain a few sentences from other letters of Saint Paul : but, in general, they presuppose a state of the Church much more definitely organized than in the time of Paul's literary activity. The Epistle to the Ephesians, as we have it, is evidently an attempt to bring Paul on the scene of second-century problems, just as the book of Daniel was an attempt to bring the prophet Daniel of the captivity on the scene of the Maccabean struggle. But it must be confessed that the resemblances of Ephesians and Colossians furnish the critics with some of their most difficult problems. Holtzmann, one of the ablest of them, has worked out the idea that the two Epistles are daring variations on some theme of Paul's,— a short Epistle of his to the Colossians. One thing is sure : if the two Epistles are not Paul's, they are Pauline,— natural continuations of his thought upon that line which made him a favorite with the Gnostics of the second century, and suspected by orthodox Christians.

Strangely enough it was in 1835 that Baur published his work on the Pastoral Epistles, assigning them to the second century. I say " strangely enough," because in 1835 Vatke published his " Religion of the Old Testament " ; and, as he proposed to work out from the *terra firma* of the prophets into the unknown regions round about, so did Baur propose to work out from Paul's known Epistles into the rest of the New Testament, making the tendency of each particular book with reference to the differences between Peter and Paul the test of its chronology. This is why the criticism of Baur and his followers of the Tübingen school has been called the "tendency" criticism. Unquestionably, this method has been overworked. But, when every proper abatement has been made, it remains as central and interpretative to the New Testament as the tendency to a priestly or prophetic standpoint is to the old : like that, marshalling the different books the way that they should go ; and, like that, giving a splendor of dramatic interest to the whole body of literature in question which it never had before.

To speak briefly of the other Epistles,— those ascribed to John, Peter, James, and Jude,— that of Jude is an attempt to give the authority of Jude, or Judas, a brother of Jesus, to certain strictures on the Gnostic heresies of the second century, midway of which it probably appeared. Similarly, the Epistle of James is an attempt to give the authority of James, the brother of Jesus, to certain strictures on the Pauline doctrine of salvation by faith. It contains excellent matter, and is, moreover, interesting as an example of the Wisdom literature in the New Testament, a New Testament book of Proverbs or Wisdom of Solomon. The relation to the Fourth Gospel of the three Epistles ascribed to John is their most interesting feature. The first of these, if not written by the author of the Fourth Gospel, was written in his manner and spirit, to confound the Gnostic heretics of the second century. Even the early Church, so little critical, doubted whether the second letter of John should be included in the Canon. It is put forth as John's, but is evidently none of his, nor even by the author of the Fourth Gospel and First Epistle, of which Epistle it is a mere echo. The early Church doubted the Third Epistle also, and quite properly. As the Second Epistle is imitative of the first, so this is imitative of the second. But it is a nice little " mémoire pour servir." It shows us as by a flashlight to what hard treatment some of the evangelists of the early Church were subjected.

There are two Epistles ascribed to Peter, in neither of which had that apostle any hand. The first was written in the time of Trajan (98–117 A.D.), and reflects the terrors of the edicts issued by him against the Christians. The second of these Epistles is probably the latest book of the New Testament, written well along the third quarter of the second century, when the hope of Christ's return was dying out, and people were saying : "Where is the promise of his coming? For, since the fathers fell asleep, all things remain as they were from the beginning." Evidently, it was already quite a while "since the fathers fell asleep." But the letter is very serviceable as showing some good man at work to heal the breach between Peter and Paul, and make them seem as much alike as possible.

But the New Testament book which addresses itself *par excellence* to this task is the book of Acts. From the same hand as the Third Gospel, it enables us to see how little critical was the temper of the most critical of the New Testament writers. Read the introduction to Luke, and you will see that, "inasmuch as many had taken in hand" to write the life of Jesus, this writer proposes to write something more accurate. And yet in Luke he puts the ascension of Jesus on the day of his resurrection ; and, in Acts, without explanation or apology, forty days after. It is a most interesting book, so full of brave adventures that it has been called "the Christian Odyssey." Reading it carefully, you will notice that in one place the person changes from the third to the first; and we read "we" did so and so. In that "we" passage we have apparently our only contemporaneous historical document in the New Testament. But, as a whole, the book is a deliberate perversion of the apostolic history. The book appeared obedient to an impulse to make up the difference between Peter and Paul, to smooth over the scandal of their opposing theories and aims. But either Paul did not know his own mind and his own experience, or we have no faithful representation of him in the Acts of the Apostles. Both he and Peter are made over there : Peter is Paulinized, and Paul is Petrinized. Paul is about as narrow as Peter, and Peter almost or quite as broad as Paul. But, however cautiously the book is to be taken as a history of the time of the apostles, it is invaluable as an illustration of the methods by which the Church consolidated herself in the last decades of the second century, and stopped the mouths of heretics and schismatics.

And now, if I remember rightly, I have spoken deliberately or incidentally of every book in the New Testament except the last, as they are commonly arranged, the Apocalypse, or "Revelation of Saint John the Divine." This formerly was the impregnable fort of John, from which the authenticity of the Fourth Gospel was battered down. At least, it was pretty generally agreed, by all those who were at all disposed to see things as they are, that John, "the beloved disciple," could not have written both the Gospel and the Apocalyse; but some held fast by the former, and some by the latter. The problem was beset with many difficulties, and still is; but there are those who think they have been satisfactorily resolved by the discovery that the basis of the composition is a Jewish Apocalypse of 69 A.D., made over by Christian editors to suit their ideas and purposes in the course of the next fifty years.

It is an interesting fact that the great German critic Harnack, who had, as it were, given bonds to accept no such theory, was convinced of its soundness by his own pupil, Vischer. "The proffered solution came upon me," he writes, "as the egg of Columbus." Once done, nothing could be more simple and self-evident. Dr. Martineau has accepted this solution with almost hilarious joy. "How strange," he says, "that we should ever have thought it possible for a personal attendant on the ministry of Jesus to write or edit a book in which Jesus leads the war-march and treads the wine-press of the wrath of God till the deluge of blood rises to the horses' bits!"

Some of you will remember that I questioned Professor Toy upon this point last Sunday evening, and that he spoke of the result as still in doubt; but afterward, in private conversation, I found that his inclination to the new theory was unmistakable. Whenever, wherever, and by whomsoever the Apocalypse was written, it is most unchristian in its spirit. As for its predictions, they refer to an immediate future, and embody the superstitious fancy of the time, that the Emperor Nero was not dead, and that he was coming back to reign a second time. From first to last many pious souls have found great satisfaction in identifying their political and religious enemies with "the Scarlet Woman" and "the False Prophet" and "the Beast." It will be long before the book furnishes no entertainment of this sort. "Bray a fool in a mortar with a pestle, yet will not his foolishness depart from him."

The Higher Criticism of the New Testament has encountered some of its most serious problems in the processes which determined the formation of the New Testament Canon, the list of New Testament books as we now have them. These processes were of long duration. Not until the sixth century was there universal agreement on this list of books to the exclusion of all others. At first the Old Testament was the only sacred scripture of the Christian Church. Gradually, the New Testament books came to enjoy an equal reverence with those of the Old Testament; and, finally, the Old Testament books were forced into a secondary rank.

It is a very interesting fact that the first New Testament of which we have any knowledge was in heretical keeping,— that of the Gnostic Marcion, whose list of books comprised some ten of Paul's Epistles and a single Gospel, evidently our Luke, but with a difference, making it even more Pauline than is our version. The first orthodox collection (that of Justin Martyr, 147–160 A.D.) was very different from Marcion's. It omitted all of Paul's Epistles, and had three Gospels (our Synoptics, probably), and possibly the fourth, but with no idea of its being John's. But, as we say the devil must not have all the good tunes, so the Church said the heretics must not have all the good books or even so many as Paul's Epistles, more or less. Thereupon it laid claim to these and the four Gospels, and, in order to make this conjunction less awkward, took the book of Acts, and set it between them as the interpreter of their mutual relations. The so-called Catholic Epistles of James, John, and Peter took their several places in the New Testament, obedient to the same impulse.

In short, whenever, wherever, and by whomsoever the New Testament books were written, the principle of natural selection which determined on those we now have as the fittest to survive was the practical necessity of the growing Church to meet and combat certain developments of thought, Gnosticism and Montanism pre-eminently, that were threatening her very life. But the growing Church had no geographical or political unity; and throughout the third century, and fourth and fifth, the decisions here and there as to what books constituted the New Testament varied through a considerable range. Even when all that we now have were included, there were others which were given up with great reluctance. Not until 495 A.D. did a papal edict decide upon those we now have, and no others. But not all the local churches conformed at once to this decision.

Here is the true story of the making of a book of which the majority of Christian people still speak as if it were written by God's own hand, and given out at the beginning of our Christian history. It was four hundred and fifty years in the making, and there is not the ghost of a suspicion anywhere discoverable that the process of manufacture had any superhuman oversight or inspiration. The incongruity between these facts (which every scholar knows, and every clergyman whose education is not shamefully imperfect) and the claims made for the New Testament everywhere in orthodox circles is a scandal of such proportions that the worst scandals of our politics are altogether sweet and lovely in comparison.

The Higher Criticism of the Old Testament explains the evolution of a national religion from a miserable fetichism to the worship of one universal God. The Higher Criticism of the New Testament gives us another evolution,— the evolution of Jesus as an ideal conception, beginning with the pure humanity of the Synoptic Gospels and ascending by degrees through the earlier and later Epistles of Saint Paul until it reaches its climax in the Fourth Gospel, where, as the Eternal Logos, though infinitely more than man, he is not yet identical or commensurate with God. It is to invert all the methods of interpretation which we use elsewhere, to hesitate for a moment to accept the obvious conclusion which these premises involve. But you will find apologists who, while conceding the evolution, as they must, insist that it was an evolution of the Church's progressive appreciation of the true nature of Jesus ; some say, of progressive revelation. Miserable subterfuges these (the last a monstrous one), by which men endeavor to evade the truth that in the New Testament we have the earlier stages of that irrational deification of the human Jesus which culminated at Nicæa in 325 A.D. If there is one constructive achievement of New Testament criticism that is more obvious than any other, it is the pure humanity of Jesus, the natural and inevitable relation of his thought and work to the time and place which made the circumstantial setting of his life and death.

But the grand achievement of the Higher Criticism is not a separate synthesis of Old Testament and New: it is a synthesis including both in its majestic sweep. There is no break in the development from the fetichism of the early Hebrews to the filial and fraternal heart on which the loved disciple leaned. And the development is as strictly human as that of any child from its first infant feebleness to the maturity of all its powers. Human, but not therefore any less divine ; for there is nothing without God. And why endeavor to make it appear otherwise than so? Why stretch out the hands to save "the sifted sediment of a residuum" when a cup of blessing, full to overflowing, is so near? There is a kind of atheism in the endeavor to save some special aspect of the world to God, as if all things and persons and events were not the channels of his boundless grace.

> " Henceforth my heart shall sigh no more
> For olden time and holier shore :
> God's love and blessing, then and there,
> Are now and here and everywhere."

THE DARING HOPE.

STRICTLY speaking the Easter argument from the resurrection of Jesus from the dead is not an argument for the immortality of the soul, but for the resurrection of the body. So it has been always understood in popular thought and feeling, which are much more sincere and logical than the careful afterthoughts of compromising theologians. Disembodied spirits have never yet been the desired of all nations nor of many individuals. The people who call themselves Spiritualists are as concrete as possible in their descriptions of the spiritual world. Tennyson expresses the almost universal aspiration, when he cries,—

> "Eternal form shall still divide
> The eternal soul from all beside;
> And I shall know him when we meet."

It is this aspect of the argument from the resurrection of Jesus which has commended it to the majority. If it proves anything, it proves this. The argument is, of course, beset with difficulties. A single resurrection from the dead, however well established, seems hardly adequate to establish the resurrection of the innumerable millions of mankind whose bodies have returned to the earth during a period of some five hundred thousand years. It was only a few Christians who were to be raised at first, but gradually more and more, and finally the dead of all the innumerable years. The new anthropology, carrying back human life some half a million years, made the induction of a general resurrection from a single fact much more precarious. A little pyramid upon its apex does not impress the imagination as so unstable as one to which that of Cheops were a baby's toy. Such an inverted pyramid is the argument from the resurrection of Jesus to the general resurrection of mankind.

Then, too, the argument is a complete *non sequitur*. The resurrection of Jesus is argued from his superhuman charac-ter, his deity. Now what man has done man may do, but not what God has done. Either the argument from the resurrection of Jesus proceeds upon the ground of his humanity or it proves simply and only the resurrection of Jesus.

But, before the resurrection of Jesus can prove anything whatever, it must itself be proved. Before we can work it as a cause, we must find it as an effect. A distinguished clergyman of our own city has declared it to be "the best attested fact of ancient history." That would be thorough-going historical scepticism if Dr. Abbott had not forgotten that, in proportion to the departure of any fact from our habitual experience, it requires more evidence for our be-lief. Dr. Abbott proceeds on the assumption that the same evidence which would justify us in believing that the sun rose in the east on such or such a day would justify us in believing that it rose in the west. The resurrection of any one from the dead is exceptional in the ratio of one to some thousands of millions. Consequently, to accept it as historic truth, we should have evidence some thousands of millions times stronger than for such a fact as the birth or death of a man at such or such a time. As it is, the evi-dence for the resurrection of Jesus does not seem to me sufficient for our belief, were it merely any important but entirely probable event. I would not go over to New York to meet a friend at the station with no more reason to believe that I should find him than I have reason to believe that the resurrection of Jesus, waiving its supernatural char-acter, actually happened.

Doubtless to some of you it will seem ungracious that I should make this prelude to my discourse upon this joyous holiday. But, surely, I could do no less. If I am to speak of immortality with intellectual seriousness, I must first divest myself of all complicity with the prevailing superstition. I cannot without apology, nor without some misgivings, take for my subject one so solemn and august as the daring hope of an immortal life without protesting earnestly against the stupendous folly (I had almost said the stupendous wickedness) of entangling such a hope with an event of infinitely doubtful authenticity and significance, which happened or did not happen some two thousand years ago. Men must care vastly less for immortality than for some plausible construction of a traditional opinion who can use their strength in trying to secure for that opinion a longer lease of life, and the chief place among the reasons for believing in a future state.

Theology has berated science roundly for its inadequacy in the spiritual realm ; but, in truth, the methods of its own protagonists have had in them some scientific implication. Theology has been sensational with the sensational philosophers, and transcendental with the transcendentalists. For a sensational philosophy the argument from the resurrection of Jesus was as sensational as it could ask. It argued the immortality of the soul (or at least the resurrection of the body) from the physical resurrection of Jesus from the grave two days after his burial.* The content of the argument was supernatural ; but its method was scientific,— not soundly and securely so, but still scientific. It argued from one concrete phenomenon to another. So far, so good. But it argued from a particular to a universal, of all fallacies the most preposterous. I speak of this only to show that the least scientific are often more scientific than they think. Because their science is hasty and imperfect science, it does not cease to be science. We do not think of excluding the earlier geologists and biologists from the great hall of science because they were not as accurate as Darwin and Huxley, who in their turn will have to be revised.

A much more scientific method than that of the theologians, arguing from the resurrection of Jesus to a universal

* Thirty-six hours. The traditional three days cannot possibly be made out.

resurrection, is that of the Spiritualists, arguing from their
"phenomena" to the reality of a spiritual world.   Some of
these also you will find decrying science.   Science, they tell
you, deals with matter, and can know nothing about spirit.
But the word "phenomena" is, *par excellence*, a scientific
word.   It is the reproach flung at science by metaphysics
that it knows nothing but phenomena.   The phenomena of
science are sensuous appearances.   So are the phenomena
of the Spiritualist.   They appeal to eye and ear and touch.
The wiser Spiritualists not only admit, but boast that their
method is scientific.   It *is* so, but not always so rigorously
so as it might be.   The scientific Spiritualist is confronted
by certain facts.   First, he makes sure that they are facts.
He eliminates the element of fraud.   Then he endeavors to
explain the facts.   The new psychology enables him to explain a dozen now where he could not explain one a few
years ago without resort to the hypothesis of extra-mundane
interference.   The range of this hypothesis has been indefinitely narrowed by our new studies in hypnotism, unconscious cerebration, the subconscious mind, telepathy, and so
on.*   But there are men who do not wish to be deceived,
men who are resolved to deal sternly with the phenomena,
who find a small residuum which they cannot eliminate and
to which they feel obliged to give an extra-mundane explanation.   These men are truly scientific.   But you will notice
that they offer us no proof of immortality.   They simply
prove that certain phenomena are without ordinary, or even
extraordinary and yet natural, explanation.   Then they say,
Assuming immortality, these things could be accounted for.
But all that is proved is that we have certain inexplicable
facts.   The case is similar to that of the perturbations of
the planet Uranus.   The astronomer determined that another planet of a certain size would cause those perturbations.   Then he turned his telescope to the spot where such
a planet should be, and there it was.   But the Spiritualist

---

* The argument *for* Spiritualism from these things is certainly unsound.   Surely they
make it likelier that the "phenomena" are produced by subtle interrelations of people in
this world.

has no telescope with which to verify his theory. Nay, but indeed he has. Our name for it is — death. Dying, the Spiritualist will discover if his Neptune, too, is there. He cannot know till then.

I have called the hope of immortality a daring hope because, for one thing, it goes so in the teeth of the appearance of the soul's implication with the fortunes of the body, and for another thing because it is a daring thing to hope for the responsibilities of an everlasting life. As for the soul's implication with the fortunes of the body, it is so intimate that it cannot be exaggerated. So testifies a recent thinker, whose confidence that the intimacy is not identity is absolutely perfect and entire, wanting nothing. But, where the intimacy is so intense, it surely is not strange that many think it means identity. Where the mind is so powerfully and seriously affected by bodily changes, it is not strange that the great change which we call death should seem to mean the ruin of the tenant with the house. How dare to hope for immortality when in the presence of our dead there is absolutely nothing to suggest that anything remains of them except the impassive form which soon will be resolved into the earth from which its constituent parts were drawn?

As for men's daring to assume the vast responsibility of an eternal life, it must be said that many, when the matter is presented to them in this way, draw back from it affrighted and appalled. But it does not often so present itself; and, where it does, the most of us are so weak in our imagination that the conception of eternal life is a mere verbal form, containing little thought. For the most part, the idea is that we want more life than we have, or can have, in this mundane sphere. We may be ready in some dim hereafter to lay down the burden of our life : we are not ready yet. Like Tennyson,

> " We seek at least

> " Upon the last and sharpest height,
> Before the spirits fade away,
> Some landing-place to clasp, and say :
> ' Farewell ! We lose ourselves in light.' "

But what if time and space are, as the idealist declares, only the forms in which we pour the molten substance of our thought, as that thought is conditioned now and here ? Or, even if they persist, who cannot easily imagine that we may live a life so full of thought and love that to us, as to the Eternal, a thousand years shall be as one day ? What do we know of time or space here in this present life, when we are at the top of our condition ? Are there not hours of thought and love that are not so long as minutes of mere drudgery or vacancy ? May we not dare to hope that some such principle as this, when charactered in heavenly form, will make the burden of our immortality as little burden-some as are an eagle's wings,—

> " Where he will, swooping downward ;
> Where he will, soaring onward " ?

The hope of immortality would indeed be a daring hope if, its appeal to a concrete sensuous appearance (the resurrection of Jesus) proving utterly vain, and the phenomena of the Spiritualist not being available for one reason or another, or not satisfactory, the case against immortality from the standpoint of science were as complete and damaging as it has been represented by the traditional theologians and apologists of recent times. But you will notice that their representation has been like that of men with lawn-mowers and bicycles or daily newspapers to sell,— they depreciate the rival article. The supernaturalist has done his best to depreciate all rational arguments for immortality, if haply so men might be obliged to come to him for it and pay his price. It was only yesterday that our Unitarian fathers were as deep in the mud of this business as were the other churches in the mire. One of our most distinguished preachers, whose father was a preacher before him, tells me that, in looking over his father's sermons, he was as-tonished to find him continually minimizing reason and science in order to maximize revelation. I do not see why he should have been astonished. That motley was pretty

much the only wear some fifty years ago; and there are still
suits of it in good repair, or tatters, which are worn by theologians of great local reputation, here and there. Their
argument is an *argumentum ad terrorem :* You've got to take
the belief in immortality upon our terms, because you can't
have it upon any other.

It is not at all strange that science has as yet done little
to confirm men's hope of an immortal life. So long as the
traditional ideas held their own, the fifth wheel to a coach
was not more superfluous than any scientific argument.
Why add a farthing candle's sputtering gleam to the ineffable splendor of the sun? With an infallible revelation of
immortality in the New Testament, why spend a moment in
endeavoring to work out some rational argument? This
was the line taken by the dogmatists, while as yet their
dogma remained unimpeached. But, when men began to
impeach it, then the scientific temper was depreciated, in
order to make the supernatural dogma seem impressive in
comparison with the scantiness of the scientific argument.
When we consider these things, and how short the time
since any serious scientific interest in immortality began, the
wonder is to me, not that the scientific argument is so
incomplete, but that it possesses so many elements of
enduring strength already, and has so much of glorious
promise in its eyes.

Consider with me some of those particulars in which the
development of science tends to make the hope of immortality less daring than it was, more reasonable; but first a
few considerations of a more general character. One of
these, and not the least important, is the vast accession we
have had to our persuasion of the unspeakable wonder of
the universe. Telescope and microscope have maintained
a generous rivalry in this regard. Innumerable experiments
and observations have brought their glory and honor into
the grand result. Hence a universe vastly more wonderful
than that formerly conceived. But what has this to do with
immortality? Much every way. To hope for it is to

"fetch our eyes up to God's style and manners of the sky."
The wonderfulness of immortality suits the wonderfulness
of the great whole. And this makes many things seem
possible which could not seem so formerly. The more
wonderful immortality, now, the more likely its reality,
responding to our hope and need.

But in the wonder of science there inheres one awful
prophecy. It is that ultimately this whole earth of ours will
be as lifeless and forlorn as those strange regions of the
farthest north into which the Norwegian "Fram" pushed
her adventurous prow. There will come a time, we read,
when the moon that makes our nights so beautiful will come
ricochetting across the surface of the earth, ploughing it
fathoms deep. Like the old lady who was told that Univer-
salism had abolished hell, "I hope for better things." But
the consensus of the competent tends to anticipate some
such catastrophe, and I submit that we have here a negative
suggestion of immortality of first-rate importance. Given an
earth forever swinging joyously upon her way and the idea
of a social immortality, the idea of George Eliot's "Choir
Invisible," might be sufficient for our aspiration and our
hope. But this idea is negatived by the prophecy of the
cessation of human life upon the earth. And hence it
seems that, if our human thought has any slightest correspondence with the eternal verities, there must be an immortal individuality to conserve the long result of time. I
would not say that the whole human course is worse than
wasted if there be no immortal conservation of its energy.
But, if I would not play the fool in order that I may justify
the ways of God, I must say that a depopulated earth
without soul-immortality would be an anticlimax of immense
irrationality, "a tale told by an idiot, full of sound and
fury, signifying " — what?

One other general consideration that contributes not a
little to our daring hope, or at least clears the ground for
it to build upon. It is that, in the region of things dead and
done for, materialism is as conspicuous as Lucifer in Mil-

ton's hell. Not long ago materialism seemed to have the middle of the road. Now it is pushed against the side, over the edge, and into the abyss of things discredited. Science and philosophy are perfectly agreed that this is so. And why? Because it is so evident that all that we know of matter is some form of our own consciousness. It is only mind of which we know anything by first intention. No one has ever seen an atom. There are two millions of these hypothetic particles of Dalton in the minimum visible of the microscope. If we could isolate one of them, and with a microscope two thousand times more powerful than the most powerful of to-day, see this marvellous little thing, we should be as much as ever in an ideal world. Certain sensations of color and form and hardness would be our utmost goal. Now this evident superiority of mind to matter and resolution of matter into mind, to a very great extent, are certainly calculated to diminish the terrors of matter as a "commensurate antagonist" of the spiritual self. The materialist talked so loudly about matter as the real thing, the thing we know about, that he fairly scared us into taking things at his value. But it turns out that matter is the unreal thing, the thing that eludes us when we try to pin it down ; that what we really know about, and all we really know about, is thought, is mind. This we know directly, and matter only as "a kind of a sort of a something" which we infer as the substance causing our sensations.

And yet one other general consideration, one of first-rate importance : the thing that we are surest of and the thing of greatest permanence in the whole range of our experience is that which we express by the capital letter " I." And just here, to make sure that my wish is not fathering my thought, and that I am not taking up with the opinion of any mushy sentimentalist or half-cast theologian, I will quote the words of Fitzjames Stephen, about the hardest-headed man with whom I have any intellectual acquaintance, a great English jurist, and a man profoundly sceptical, attaching no value to the claims of Christian supernaturalism, and scrutinizing those of rational religion of whatever kind with hard severity. The quotation is a long one, but I think that it can justify itself at your tribunal both on account of its intrinsic merit and on account of the peculiar source from which it is derived. It is as follows: "All human language, all human observation, implies that the mind, the 'I,' is a thing in itself; a fixed point in the midst of a world of change, of which world of change its own organs form a part. It is the same yesterday, to-day, and to-morrow. It was what it was when its organs were of a different shape, and consisted of different matter from their present shape and matter. It will be what it is when they have gone through other changes. I do not say that this proves, but surely it suggests, it renders probable, the belief that this ultimate fact, this starting-point of all knowledge, thought, feeling, and language, 'this final inexplicability' (an emphatic though a clumsy phrase), is independent of its organs; that it may have existed before they were collected out of the elements, and may continue to exist after they are dissolved into the elements. The belief thus suggested by the most intimate, the most abiding, the most wide spread of all experiences, not to say by universal experience, as recorded by nearly every word of every language in the world, is what I mean by a belief in a future state, if indeed it should not rather be called a past, present, and future state all in one,— a state which rises above and transcends time and change. I do not say that this is proved: but I do say that it is strongly suggested by the one item of knowledge which rises above logic, argument, language, sensation, and even direct thought, that one clear instance of direct consciousness in virtue of which we say, 'I am.' This belief is that there is in man, or rather that man is, that which rises above words and above thoughts, which are but unuttered words; that to each one of us, 'I' is the ultimate central fact which renders thought and language possible." Here endeth the quotation, and I do not wish to press it on you for more than it is worth. I do not ask you to accept this

persistency of self-consciousness through a life of seventy or
eighty years and all manner of physical changes and vicissi-
tudes, the body's growth, the body's slow decay, as a proof
of its superiority to death itself; but, surely, you will all
agree with me that this persistency suggests with overwhelm-
ing force that it is the things that are seen which are transient, the things that are unseen that are permanent.

> "The hills are shadows, and they flow
> From form to form, and nothing stands;
> They melt like mist, the solid lands;
> Like clouds they shape themselves and go."

But what does not flow from form to form, what does not
melt like mist, what does not shape itself and go, is this
inexpugnable, ineradicable I, this self-consciousness which
no metaphysical analysis can disintegrate or destroy. And
we have here, it seems to me, a rejoinder of the most crushing weight to that popular imagination or materialistic
theory which finds in things spiritual the impermanent and
transitory and in things material such as are relatively fixed
and strong.

All these considerations are general; and, as I have said,
they do but clear the way for those of a more positive
nature, make, as it were, a sky, an atmosphere, on which
a positive argument can unfold its wings and trust itself to
the illimitable air. So far, I have done little more than
show that some of the ordinary presumptions against immortality are wholly invalid, and indeed, when thoroughly
examined, yield conclusions quite the opposite of those
habitually drawn. But, of those considerations of a more
positive nature which science yields, I will name two only;
and on these I need not dwell, because I have more than
once before now told you how much they mean to me.
Here, I believe, are two "natural laws in the spiritual world"
which Mr. Henry Drummond did not name; and yet I am
persuaded that they are more valid and important than any
named by that lamented writer in his fallacious and mis-

leading book. One of them is the conservation of energy. It may well be doubted if this, and not natural selection or evolution, is not the great scientific doctrine of the century. It is a natural law of quite immeasurable significance. Is it also a spiritual law? No physical force is ever lost. It is conserved even where it is most widely dissipated, and reappears in other forms. How is it with that energy which we call the soul, which we call Shakspere or Newton or Lincoln, which we call wife or mother, husband or child or friend? What conservation is there of the energy that was in these, in what remains of them to bury in the earth or burn with fire, after the last farewells? The question comes home to us as pointedly from any grave where humblest worth lies buried as from the splendid mausoleum where a grateful nation lavishly enshrines her mighty dead. If the conservation of energy is a law which stops short at the bounds of matter, then there is nothing more to say; but, if it is a law of matter *and of spirit*, then must we believe that somehow, somewhere, not only the mighty ones of intellect and imagination, but those who had a genius for affection and devotion, will live again, a conscious individual life. And, mind you, those who can find nothing in man but the material are bound, as are no others, to subscribe to this. If the soul is a material commodity, what conservation is there of its energy in the solids, liquids, gases, into which the body is resolved? Can these write immortal poems, save nations from destruction, divinize the most humble life with the supreme significance of love? No, they cannot; and, if the conservation of energy is a natural law in the spiritual world, then have we a suggestion of the utmost dignity and importance that death does not end all.

But there is another natural law in which I find another argument for immortality. It is the law of vital correlation. Let me explain. In the development of animal structures there goes along with the development of special organs, parts, and functions the development of certain others, adapting the animal structures to changed conditions. Now in the spiritual life of man there goes along with all that is best in his intelligence, noblest in his affections, grandest and sweetest in his moral nature, the development of the hope of an immortal life. Of course, we have our moments when the pulse of life is slack, and we imagine that we should prefer eternal sleep to any wakening. But I am speaking of the normal man, not of the slack-twisted and down-hearted. And here, at the top of our condition, is a correlated growth ; and, if the hope which is thus developed correlatively with our noblest living is not a solemn and majestic portent of a sublime reality, then have we a radical contradiction in our nature, every higher thought or nobler act or purer purpose tending to immerse us deeper in a terrible illusion. It is the same Power which organizes in us the purest splendors of our thought and love which organizes in us correlatively the hope of immortality, so that if, in very deed and truth, "it is impossible for God to lie," that hope must mean its realization as surely as the earth's revolution on its axis means alternate night and day.

But I would not make too much of these considerations. Let Science do all that she can — it is much more than I have said — for us, and still our best resource will be a daring hope. If the most and best of science are but little, then the hope is all the more daring, and no worse on that account. Our relations to a conscious individual life hereafter would lose the finest essence of their religious character if the Spiritualist or anybody else could give us a complete scientific demonstration. That finest essence is the precipitation of ourselves upon our hope,— not nourishing that in any deliberate fashion, but simply living our best life, and then, if that life flowers into a great fragrant hope, daring to cherish it, though all the arguments of science seem to press the other way.

We read in Nansen's "Farthest North"—a book that expands our faith in human nature more than our knowledge of the northern seas — that, when the vessel was drifting south or too much west, the men were dispirited and sad ;

but, when she was moving onward toward the unknown
world, their hearts were always glad. If we are not so
impatient of the winds and tides which hold us back from
the unknown as were Nansen's men, I would that we might
be as fearless as were they of the unknown. And, indeed, I
am persuaded that, the further on we go, the more we leave
behind us of familiar things, and the stranger the new aspects of the sea and sky, the quieter become our hearts.

> "Naked from out that far abyss behind us
>   We entered here.
> No word came with our coming to remind us
>   What wondrous world was near,—
>   No hope, no fear.

> "Into the silent, starless night before us
>   Naked we glide.
> No hand has mapped the constellations o'er us,
>   No comrade at our side,
>   No chart, no guide.

> "Yet, fearless, toward that midnight, black and hollow,
>   Our footsteps fare.
> The beckoning of a Father's hand we follow,—
>   His love alone is there."
>   *And that we dare.*